RIGGED JUSTICE

RIGGED JUSTICE

HOW THE COLLEGE ADMISSIONS SCANDAL RUINED AN INNOCENT MAN'S LIFE

JOHN VANDEMOER

HarperOne
An Imprint of HarperCollinsPublishers

HarperCollins books may be purchased for educational, business, or sales promotional use. For information, please email the Special Markets Department at SPsales@harpercollins.com.

FIRST EDITION

Designed by Nancy Singer

Library of Congress Cataloging-in-Publication Data

Names: Vandemoer, John, author.
Title: Rigged justice : how the college admissions scandal ruined an innocent man's life / John Vandemoer.
Description: First HarperOne Hardcover Edition. | New York : HarperOne, [2021]
Identifiers: LCCN 2021010912 (print) | LCCN 2021010913 (ebook) | ISBN 9780063020108 (Hardback) | ISBN 9780063020122 (eBook)
Subjects: LCSH: Universities and colleges—United States—Admission—Corrupt practices. | Universities and colleges—United States—Administration. | Vandemoer, John. | Stanford University—Sports—History.
Classification: LCC LB2351 .V36 2021 (print) | LCC LB2351 (ebook) | DDC 378.1/61—dc23
LC record available at https://lccn.loc.gov/2021010912
LC ebook record available at https://lccn.loc.gov/2021010913

21 22 23 24 25   LSC   10 9 8 7 6 5 4 3 2 1

This is a work of nonfiction. The events and experiences I detail here are all true and have been faithfully rendered as I remember them, to the best of my ability. Though conversations come from my keen recollection, I did not write them to represent word-for-word documentation; rather, I have retold them in a way that evokes the real feeling and meaning of what was said. Three phone conversations between Rick Singer and me in October 2018 were taken from partial transcripts created by the FBI and presented in court documents. Statements made in open court were taken from transcripts of the proceedings. In addition, the names of two students in the book, Bodhi Patel and Mia D'Angelo, have been changed to protect the privacy of these two individuals. Finally, Stanford athletics director Bernard Muir has publicly denied that he personally knows Rick Singer.

To Molly, Nicholas, and Nora

1

You probably don't think you need to hear this. I wouldn't have guessed I did. But here's the thing: when special agents from the Internal Revenue Service and Federal Bureau of Investigation knock on your door at 7 a.m. and flash their badges and ask whether they can come in, your answer should be no. Tell them you're happy to reschedule when you have a lawyer by your side.

Maybe that knock will come, as it did for me, after you have just finished changing your daughter's diaper, and the remnants of your kids' breakfasts—yogurt and smashed berries—are all over your Red Sox T-shirt and pajama pants. Maybe you and your wife will be in the middle of snapping onesies and tying shoes and packing backpacks so you can get to daycare drop-off before you both rush off to work. You're going to be puzzled by the agents' appearance on your front step and probably a little nervous—I know I was—and your instinct will be to say, "Sure, of course, come in."

You may even offer them coffee and help with their chairs as they settle in at your kitchen table. Then you'll join them and fold your hands in front of you and look at them openly, ready to help. You'll think you are doing the right thing—after all, you have nothing to hide—but you will be making a colossal mistake.

Only innocent people let them in, my lawyer would tell me later. Criminals know not to do that.

But there they were, sitting across from each other: two federal agents, both female, both around thirty years old, both in gray pantsuits—all business. The IRS agent, who had introduced herself as Elizabeth Keating, had placed a blank yellow legal pad and a pen in front of her. The other woman, from the FBI, whose name I did not catch, had pulled a stapled packet of papers out of a portfolio. From where I was sitting at the end of the oval table, I could make out a few words on the top page. I saw my name. I saw "Stanford University."

"So, we just want to confirm a few things with you," the FBI agent said. "You are John Vandemoer."

I heard Boston in her pronunciation. *Vanda-moah.*

"You are the head sailing coach at Stanford."

"Yes," I said.

"Beautiful school. Must be nice living here right on campus?"

"It is. Yes. It's great."

My wife, Molly, and I had moved to this development of spacious, two-story houses built by Stanford for its coaching staff seven years before. We'd brought each of our two children home from Stanford's Children's Hospital after they'd been born, and now they were enrolled in a terrific on-campus daycare center a few blocks from our house. Our fellow coaches were our neighbors and friends. We went to each other's competitions, cheered each other's successes, and celebrated holidays and birthdays together. Molly and I loved the community and life we'd built here.

"Now, part of your job, Mr. Vandemoer is recruiting athletes for the sailing team. Is that correct?"

"That's right."

"Would you walk us through that a little? How recruiting works at Stanford?"

I started in on the basics—that academics were the primary consideration, that there were no scholarships in college sailing, and that my sport wasn't part of the National Collegiate Athletic Association (NCAA), so I wasn't under those constraints. I told them that Stanford admissions allotted me six or seven slots for recruited sailors each year, provided those students met the school's stringent academic standards. Agent Keating took notes while I spoke.

The FBI agent asked me about application timelines and test scores and GPAs, often referring to the paper in front of her as if she were reading from a script. They were the kinds of questions I'd answered happily hundreds of times at college nights and high school regattas during my eleven years at Stanford and before that, as head coach at the US Naval Academy in Maryland. Recruiting was one of my favorite parts of the job. I knew a lot of coaches who dreaded it, but I liked interacting with young athletes, learning what their strengths were, and figuring out where they might fit on the team. What I didn't enjoy was having to tell kids no. But I prided myself on being honest if I didn't see a spot for them. I never wanted to give anyone false hope.

"And when you find a student you want, what do you?" she asked, turning to the next page in her packet.

"I take their academic information to the admissions office. They're only looking at grades and test scores at that point, just the feasibility of them getting in."

"And this happens when?"

"July and August, mostly. I do it then because the Ivies can't offer kids anything until September 1st. I try to, you know, beat them to the punch."

"Makes sense," she said, giving me a fleeting smile.

I smiled back. Agent Keating didn't look up.

"And if they have the appropriate grades and scores, what happens then?"

"Then admissions might give me a pink envelope to send to them," I said.

"Pink envelope?"

"Pink envelopes are what Stanford calls early application packets that are just for recruited athletes."

I told them that Stanford usually offered me about a dozen pink envelopes for potential recruits. Receiving that application didn't guarantee the school would accept the kids, and it wasn't a promise that I'd ultimately use one of my admissions slots on them. It just meant they were over the first hurdle in the recruiting process. Sometimes, the high school students who received the pink envelopes decided not to apply to Stanford. But if they did fill out the application, those bright pink envelopes went into a special pile and got an early read from admissions officers.

"And this gives them a leg up on regular applicants?"

"To a certain extent, yes, because they've already been vetted. Admissions wouldn't offer a pink envelope to them unless they had a very good shot at getting in."

"And do you know how many of your recruits get in?"

"My acceptance rate is about 80 percent," I said.

"And the usual Stanford acceptance rate?"

"It's less than 5 percent."

She looked up at me, tilted her head, and narrowed her eyes. "Okay. So, your support does help a great deal."

I detected a hint of disapproval in her voice. I shifted in my seat. Upstairs, I could hear Nicholas repeatedly asking Molly who Daddy was talking to. Nora had started to cry. I felt terrible that Molly had to deal with the kids by herself. I glanced at my watch. It was almost 8 a.m. We both had to get to work.

"Can you tell me what this is about?" I asked.

I knew a big NCAA basketball scandal had blown up recently; recruiting rules had been violated, coaches had been fired, shoe company executives had been caught bribing athletes. It had been all over the national news. I thought they might be gathering background information for that case, getting the lay of the recruiting land, something like that.

"Just a few more questions," Agent Keating said, glancing up at me.

The FBI agent turned to another page. I spotted a familiar name. Rick Singer.

"Now, Mr. Vandemoer, I want to ask you about some donations to the sailing program," she said. "Do you remember a man by the name of Rick Singer?"

"Yes."

"And he is?"

"He's a college placement counselor I've worked with."

"And he donated to your team, did he not?"

"Yes, he did."

She asked how I met Rick Singer and how often I spoke to him. I did my best to summarize our handful of encounters since he'd first called me in 2016.

"So, what's this about?" I asked again. "Is he in some kind of trouble?"

"He might have done some bad stuff, yeah. We're just following up."

Molly and the kids came down the stairs. The two agents stayed seated while they introduced themselves. Molly said hello and then looked at me with raised eyebrows. I gave her a look to say, *No idea*.

"I'm going to take the kids now," Molly said. She had Nora in her arms and a diaper bag on her shoulder. I asked to be excused so I could help her load the stroller for the ten-minute walk to the Stanford daycare center.

"What's going on?" Molly asked when we got outside.

"I don't know." I bent down to buckle Nicholas in. "They're asking questions about that big donor, Rick Singer. I think maybe he's in trouble. I'll call you when they leave."

"Beautiful family," both women said when I sat back down at the table.

"So, we were talking about donations," the FBI agent said. "Would that be a factor in your decision to recruit if the family had the means to donate?"

"In my decision to recruit?" I said. "No, I mean, families do donate. We welcome donations, but that wouldn't—"

"Would you take money for recruits?"

"Donations?"

"How much money would you take?"

"I'm not sure what you're asking me. How much families donate?"

"What about Rick Singer? What was your arrangement with him?"

"No arrangement, really. He brought me a couple of possible recruits, but they didn't pan out."

"You had a financial arrangement with him."

"He made some donations to the team. His clients wanted to donate, and then he—"

"But you had an agreement—"

"An agreement? I don't know what you mean."

She paused and put her elbows on the table, then rubbed her temples. "I'm sorry. I'm not making myself clear." She gazed out the window to our little backyard. I sensed she was weighing her choice of words. "How much did it take for a recruit, if Singer brought a recruit . . ."

Agent Keating looked up, sighed heavily, put her pen down, and leaned toward me.

"Why . . . was Rick Singer . . . giving you money?" she asked pointedly. Her tone scared me.

"Because he believed in what I was doing," I said. "He was interested in sailing."

Singer had told me again and again how impressed he was with the Stanford sailing program and the way I ran it. He had donated because he wanted to be supportive. All the money went directly to the team coffers to help pay for coaches, equipment, and travel to regattas. I never pocketed a dollar.

"He gave you money to support his clients. To get those kids into Stanford."

"No," I said. "They were donations to the team—"

"Oh, come on, John. You were taking money for recruits. You know you were."

"What? No, no, I was—"

"Don't lie to us!" she said, raising her voice and lifting herself out of the chair so she loomed above me. "You knew it was wrong, but you took his money anyway!"

My hands had started to tremble. I put them on my lap. Why was she acting like I was a criminal? I hadn't done anything wrong.

"I didn't take any money," I said.

Agent Keating sat back down and shook her head.

The FBI agent pulled a paper out of her folder. I recognized it as a copy of a Ranking and Justification form I'd written last summer that included brief notes about each of the recruits I'd been considering at the time. I edited the list from week to week, adding or dropping candidates. I was stunned that she had that confidential memo. It was for Stanford admissions eyes only.

"What was your interest in this girl?" she said, pointing at the last name on the list. "Mia D'Angelo."

I told them Rick Singer had brought Mia to my attention as a possible recruit. She was a gymnast from Las Vegas who had done some sailing out of Newport Beach, where her family had a second home.

"She is not a sailor," she said.

"Not a top sailor, no. But I need kids at different levels to fill out my roster. They could be practice players and maybe work their way up."

"Players?"

"Players, yes. They're athletes, just like on any other team."

"Okay. So, you listed her, this potential *player*, as a recruit for the sailing team, even though she didn't sail?"

"She did sail. Not on a high school team or anything, but she sailed out of the Newport Harbor Yacht Club, and she was also training at the US Sailing Center in Long Beach. She planned to switch from gymnastics to sailing in college. Gymnasts make that shift really well."

"Mia D'Angelo does not sail. At all."

"Rick Singer told me—I don't know why he would—anyway, she didn't end up applying to Stanford. I took her off my list."

"But you didn't care that she didn't sail, did you? You would have supported her if she had applied," Agent Keating said. "Singer was paying you to do that. He gave you money to ensure that."

"No, no. He donated to Stanford, to the team."

"What about this other girl? Molly Zhao?"

"I didn't support her. She was a decent sailor, but I didn't need her."

"Singer told you she was a 'decent' sailor?"

"I saw her résumé."

"And this student? Bodhi Patel? Singer told you about him, as well?"

"Yes. He brought him to me."

"Good sailor?"

"Mediocre sailor with great grades. I considered him a long shot, maybe someone who could contribute with the right coaching."

"Oh, the right *coaching*," she said mockingly and then leaned toward me. "Not one of these students sailed, John. You knew that."

"I don't, I was told—" I swallowed hard.

"Singer gave you money for all three of these students even though they were not sailors. Isn't that true?"

"He told me they sailed. And he wanted to support my program."

"Oh, come on. You knew what you were doing was wrong. You were breaking the law!"

This was crazy. Breaking the law? I'd accepted donations for the team. It was part of my job—part of the job of coaches in every sport at Stanford. We all relied on benefactors to augment our team budgets.

"What law did I break? I don't understand."

"You were taking money for recruits," Agent Keating said forcefully, punctuating her words by jabbing a finger toward me. "That's how you were breaking the law. And you work for a school that receives federal funds."

I felt myself fighting for a shallow, ragged breath. Had I violated some obscure recruiting rule? If I had, I certainly hadn't meant to. My bosses at Stanford had been happy I'd brought in the donations. The director of athletics himself had congratulated me.

"No, I mean, if I did do something, you know, I, uh—can I just talk to Stanford about this? I think there's a misunderstanding—"

"No, absolutely not. Stanford is mad at you. They know all about this. You can't talk to them."

"What do you mean Stanford knows all about this? Why can't I talk to them?"

"It would be obstruction of justice if you speak to anyone at Stanford University. You may talk to no one about this."

"What do I—?" My voice broke. "Do I need a lawyer?"

"I do think it would be a good idea to get a lawyer, John. Yes," Agent Keating said.

"I don't know any lawyers. I can't afford a lawyer."

"We can look into getting you a public defender, see if the US Attorney in Boston will allow you to do that. You'd just have to fill out some forms."

She handed me her business card. My hand shook as I took it from her. It read, "Elizabeth Keating, Special Agent, IRS—Criminal Investigation, Boston Field Office." *Criminal Investigation.* Jesus. What was this?

"Am I being charged with something?"

"You seem like a good person," she said. Her tone had suddenly turned lighter, as if we were just wrapping up a friendly chat. "And you have a very nice family here."

"Beautiful family," the FBI agent said, sliding her papers back into her leather portfolio. She pushed back her chair to stand up.

"And you are cooperating. If you didn't let us in and you didn't cooperate, then we would have come down really hard on you," Agent Keating said. "But you did, so things will be just fine. It will be fine for you."

I didn't know it then, but that was not true. It wasn't going to be fine. It was never going to be fine again.

2

I watched them walk away, then closed the front door and stared at the back of it, trying to breathe, trying to understand what had just happened. I had to talk to Molly. I went upstairs to our bedroom, found my phone, then dropped to my knees next to the bed and called her.

"I'm freaking out," I said when she picked up. "It's not at all what I thought it was."

"Why? What did they say?"

"They said I broke the law. I have no idea what they're talking about." My throat tightened. "I don't—"

"It's okay."

"I'm really scared. They said I should get a lawyer and that they could get me one."

"Well, that's good, right, that they get you one?"

"But do you think that's weird to use a lawyer from them?"

"I don't know. We need to talk to someone who knows about this stuff."

"They told me I couldn't tell anyone."

"But a lawyer? We couldn't ask for advice?"

"I don't know. I think they said not to."

"What if I ask Anne?" Molly said. Her friend Anne Wright was on the board of the Peninsula Youth Sailing Foundation (PYSF), the non-profit youth sailing program Molly had been hired to direct in 2012 just after she'd competed in the London Olympics. Anne was married to Ian Wright, a tech CEO. "They have to know great lawyers. I could talk to her and just be really vague."

"Okay."

"We'll figure it out," Molly said. "Don't worry."

I didn't know how she was staying so calm. "I'm completely freaked out."

"I'm sure it will be fine. Can you think of anyone else we can ask?"

I had a moment of clarity and remembered an old friend from Annapolis, Scott Berenberg. He was a former State Department investigator, and his area of expertise was fraud and corruption. I would never have dreamed that I'd need to ask him for his professional advice.

"What about Scott?" I said.

"Great idea. Try him right now."

After we hung up, I texted him.

I was supposed to go to my office in the athletics building on campus that morning, but the investigators had told me not to talk to anyone, and I knew I wouldn't be able to pull off casual conversations with my fellow coaches. I decided to head straight for the Stanford boathouse, which was set on a tidal creek in Redwood City about eight miles away. The rowing team, which shared the facility, would be done for the day. My team's practice didn't start for a few hours. I could be alone.

Scott texted me back just as I pulled into the parking lot. "Call me."

I got out of the car, went around the boathouse to the waterfront, then walked out to the end of the long rowing dock. I was having trouble holding the phone steady. I told myself to be calm when Scott answered. I'd just feel him out on what, hypothetically speaking, a person might do if he found himself in a situation with federal agents.

"Johnny V! What's up?"

"Scott, you won't believe this, but the FBI came to my house this morning with the IRS, and they think I broke some recruiting law or something and this guy I know, I don't know him well, he's a donor and a college counselor, and he was sort of helping me with recruits. He's part of it, and they told me not to tell anyone, but I just—"

"Whoa—what? Okay. Tell me what happened. Start at the beginning."

I took a deep breath and told him about the agents who had come to my house.

"Classic," he said. "The early morning thing. To catch you off guard. That's what we do."

"They asked me a lot of questions about recruiting."

"And you answered?"

"Yes. Every question," I said, walking back toward the boathouse.

"Did they explain why they were there?"

"No, not really. They wanted to know about this counselor I worked with. He ended up making some big donations to the sailing program."

"Okay."

"And they were yelling at me like they thought I took that money for myself. Like I had some deal with him to get kids into Stanford. I would never do that."

"Did they say they were charging you with something?"

"I don't think so. But it was confusing. They didn't really say."

"I don't like how they did this. I mean, they don't have to read you your rights, but this is so inappropriate to get you talking before they told you why they were there."

"I'm still not sure why they were there," I said. "They said I should probably get a lawyer. They said they could get one for me. Should I do that?"

"Yeah, I think that's okay. A court-appointed lawyer has to work for you. You said these were donations? And the money went to Stanford?"

"Yes. All of it." I turned and headed back to the end of the dock.

"It doesn't sound like you broke any laws. You know what I think? I bet they want you to witness against that guy."

"You think that's it?"

"I do. I think they're pressuring you, so you'll testify."

"They do it like that—just try to scare the crap of you?"

"Yeah," he said. "For sure."

I looked back toward the boathouse and saw that Clinton Hayes and Belle Strachan, the sailing team's two assistant coaches, had arrived. They stood just inside the open garage doors of the sailboat bay and waved to me. I lifted my hand.

After our call ended, I texted Molly, who was just around the corner at PYSF. Her office was in a repurposed shipping container near the public boat ramp.

"Scott thinks they want me as a witness," I wrote.

"I thought it must be something like that," she replied.

"I feel much better."

"Me too. Have a good practice. Love you."

I still felt shaky when I went into the boathouse, but I willed myself into our routine. We did what we always did before practice: went upstairs and checked the SailFlow app to see wind speeds and current all over the Bay Area. Those readings helped us decide which drills to run and whether or not to stay in the shelter of the creek's basin or head out into the open water of South San Francisco Bay.

After we made our plan for the afternoon, Clinton and Belle left to grab a late lunch. As soon as I was alone again, a fresh wave of anxiety washed over me. What if this thing *wasn't* about me being a witness against Rick Singer? What if it was something else? I had to collect myself before my team started arriving. I left the boathouse and started down a paved walkway that skirted the creek and a complex of modern pharmaceutical company office buildings.

In a few minutes, I stopped and stared out at the mudflats and dried grass of Bair Island, the wildlife refuge that forms a natural barrier between the creek and the bay. I took a few deliberate breaths. *This is all a misunderstanding*, I told myself. *Stanford knows me.* I'd iron it all out with them. They had to know I would never do anything wrong. I looked over at the sailing center and spotted a few players arriving. It was time to head back, to greet the team with a smile.

Somehow, I got through the three-hour practice. We ran our drills and staged mock races and finished up with a team meeting in the boathouse to talk about the afternoon's takeaways and our goals for the week. Then I headed home. After Molly and I got Nicholas and Nora to bed, we sat together on the couch and I told her everything I could remember about what had happened that morning after she'd left.

"What if it's something terrible?" I said. "What if I lose my job?"

"You're not going to lose your job. If they just want you to testify, it's not like they think *you* did anything wrong. I'm sure it will be all right."

THAT NIGHT, I LAY ON MY side and stared into the darkness, thinking about Rick Singer. I tried to imagine what a lawyer might ask me about him. I had no idea how these things worked. Would Singer be in the room if I testified against him? It would be so uncomfortable to have him sitting there staring at me while I talked about him. I wondered where I would have to go to do it. What if I had to miss a practice or even a regatta? I'd have to make sure Clinton or Belle could cover for me, and that Molly had help with the kids.

Then again, maybe I wouldn't hear from those agents again. They'd decide they didn't need me. I mean, what did I know? From across the hall, I heard Nora start to cry. I got up and went to the kids' room, then picked her up and held her tight until she fell asleep again.

THE NEXT AFTERNOON, AGENT KEATING EMAILED me two forms. One was for "appointment of counsel"; the other was a financial affidavit, which was to show that I couldn't afford a lawyer. That would be easy to demonstrate. Molly's and my combined salaries were barely getting us by in Palo Alto, even with the college-subsidized housing. I started to fill out the forms, but the first few questions stumped me.

I wrote back. "What am I? A defendant? A witness? What do I write in the space that says 'Charge/Offense?' And what do I put in the blank where it says 'In the case of: U.S. Attorney v. _____'?"

She replied a few minutes later. "You can leave 'in the case of' blank. In the questions about being a defendant or a witness, check 'Other' and then write 'Unknown at this time.' In the Charge/Offense section write 'N/A.'"

N/A. That seemed promising. And apt. *Not applicable*. None of this felt even remotely applicable to me. I finished filling out the forms, then threw some clothes in my Stanford roller suitcase. I had to make a weekend trip to Florida for my other job as the Club 420 Association executive director. We put on regional and national regattas for the Club 420 class, a one-design dinghy used widely in youth sailing. The Midwinter Championship was being held in Jensen Beach, Florida.

I landed in West Palm Beach and picked up a rental car. Before I left the lot, though, I did a quick search on my phone for the closest FedEx office. I had to send my completed paperwork to the US Attorney's Office in Boston. I felt an irrational sense of relief when I dropped the packet off. All good, I told myself, as I started north for the fifty-mile trip to the venue. Off to the races.

EARLY THE NEXT MORNING, I HEADED to the US Sailing Center of Martin County, a community-run small boat training center on a broad section of the Indian River lagoon. There were trailered boats all over the lawn and walkways between the two-story yellow club-house and a small beach.

I spent the next three days onshore, shooting drone footage and doing on-camera interviews with racers for the Club 420 Association's social media sites. After the competition ended each day, I stayed through the protest period during which sailors could lodge complaints about rules infractions they said they'd experienced on the water. Each evening, after the official's rulings, I went back to my hotel, worked out in the small gym, grabbed dinner, and went to my room to edit and post my video footage. And each night, when I finally turned out the light, the anxiety that I had managed to distract myself from all day crept back in like a dense, sinister fog.

I GOT HOME MONDAY EVENING AND decided not to go into my office the next morning. I needed some time to regroup. Shortly after I got up, my phone rang. In a low, gravelly voice, the caller identified himself as John Amabile. He said he was my court-appointed lawyer.

"So first of all, I want you to know, I'm on your side. I work for you," Amabile said. "Now, do you know why this case is in Boston?"

"I don't. I hadn't even thought of that. No idea."

"And do you know what the case is about?"

"No, but I think they might want me to be a witness? Against this college recruiter I worked with."

"I see. All right. Let me call the US Attorney, see what I can find out—and then we'll go from there."

As soon as we hung up, I typed "John Amabile" into my laptop's browser. My eyes widened when I saw what came up. Amabile had been involved in several high-profile cases in Boston, including a quadruple murder dubbed the Mattapan Massacre. What was I doing with this guy? It didn't lift my spirits to read that one of Amabile's clients in that case was sentenced to four back-to-back life sentences after two trials.

A few hours later, he called again. "All right. So, John, I want to be up front with you. I'm afraid I have some bad news."

"Okay."

"I spoke to the US Attorney's Office, and it seems that you are, in fact, the target in this case. My understanding is that the government is going to say you took bribes. They have audiotapes and emails. And Mr. Singer is their witness."

I sat down hard on the sofa.

"Now, they do want to talk to us about a deal. But they said they couldn't do anything until next Tuesday, which is a bit odd. I don't know why they would be delaying it. But we won't hear anything more until next week."

"Tuesday? Next week?"

"Correct. So, what you can do now is start sending me any information you have relating to Rick Singer—emails, texts, etcetera."

"Okay."

"And don't talk to anyone about this."

I hung up and clutched my phone against my chest.

I had to get myself off the couch. I had to get to practice. I forced myself to my feet, to the shower, to the car. Somehow, I didn't side-swipe anyone on Highway 101 as I veered across two lanes of traffic at the last minute to make the Redwood City exit. I remembered that I'd said I'd stop at West Marine, a boat supply store near the sailing center, to pick up gel coat and cleaning supplies. I pulled into the parking lot, gripped the steering wheel, and stared out the windshield while the engine idled.

How could anyone think I was a criminal? The most lawless thing I'd ever done was speed on the 101. My whole life, I'd been a rule follower. I was a sailor. We prided ourselves on what was known as Corinthian spirit—the belief that sportsmanship and fair play were the most important things in competition. And for the most part, we were a self-policing sport. We were expected to own up to our mistakes. My players heard me say it day after day: nothing mattered more than honor and integrity. I'd made kids forfeit races even when they'd "gotten away" with a rules violation on the course. I told them they hadn't gotten away with anything because they knew the truth. That was not how we sailed.

I was a stickler, sometimes to a ridiculous fault. I'd once argued with Molly about taking the tags off a new mattress.

"We can't," I had said. "It says right here to not take the tag off."

"I think you can once you own it."

I pointed. "Read it. It says it's illegal."

Molly had been so exasperated she'd walked out of the room.

THE SUN BEAT ON THE CAR. I rolled down the windows and shut off the engine. I knew Amabile had said not to tell anyone about this, but I had to talk to Scott. I hit his name on my phone contacts list.

"I heard from that lawyer and it's insane. They're going—they're actually going after me." My heart was hammering. "That other guy, Rick Singer? He's their witness."

"*What?* Seriously?"

"They're saying I took bribes."

"Bribery? That makes no sense at all. You're not a government employee. I don't get that."

"He said they have some tapes or emails or something against me."

"This is outrageous. You know what? This sounds like entrapment to me. Total entrapment."

"You think so?"

"I do," he said. "I think you're going to end up making a ton of money on this."

"Really?"

"But I have to tell you; you're probably going to go through hell first."

3

When I was twelve years old—shy, overly serious, obsessed with boats—my father and I went to a breakfast gathering in our hometown of Hyannis, Massachusetts, to hear Buddy Melges speak. Melges was a sailing god—an Olympic gold medalist, a world champion, an America's Cup skipper, a boat designer, everything I dreamed of being and more. That bright morning, under a string of colorful burgees in the Hyannis Yacht Club's informal, white-washed trophy room, he had preached the gospel of wind, and I had become his spellbound disciple.

Buddy said we should sail with our whole bodies, with "all our tentacles out." He said we could learn to detect wind shifts in the fine hairs of our forearms. He told us that when the wind fizzled in the middle of a race, he liked to take off his shirt so he could sense the slightest breeze on his bare skin. We could try that, too.

"I can even smell a change in the wind," he said.

That got a few titters. He also told us that when he was a kid in Wisconsin, he would come home from school, climb a tree, and spend hours watching wind patterns as they moved across the lake he lived on. The ocean was one thing, he said, but lakes—*lakes* were where you could really learn to sail.

I felt like he was talking directly to me. My family's house was on Lake Wequaquet, one of Cape Cod's largest lakes. Next to our dock was a tall tree, perfect for climbing. After I heard Buddy speak, I went up into that old oak almost every day and parked myself in the crook of a broad limb that leaned out over the lake. I watched the way puffs ruffled and darkened patches of water, fanning out on their approach and then dissipating as they moved away. I saw how the friction created by tall trees made the breeze bend and drop with sudden force beyond the shoreline's sheltered waters. I studied how the wind funneled through the narrow opening that connected our section of the lake to the next, larger expanse; it slowed when it hit the edges of the cut and then splayed out as it exited. On days when the lake was dead calm, I turned my face skyward and sniffed, trying to channel Buddy. Could I detect something beyond those scents of sun-warmed pine needles and salt air that might signal to me that a breeze was on the way?

After a session in the tree, I'd launch my pea-green, fourteen-foot Laser and try to translate what I'd seen from above into what was happening in the boat. I started with beam reaches and broad reaches, playing with gusts and lulls, zooming across the lake with the sail eased out, getting soaked in spray. Those points of sail were fun and easy to maintain. But I was intent on mastering something more difficult to do; I wanted to get the Laser just as balanced and fast going upwind in shifty breeze. When I got it right—the mainsheet trimmed in tight, my body and rudder perfectly positioned—the boat took off like a jet. Suddenly, I wasn't fighting the tiller anymore; there seemed to be nothing in my hand at all. The boat was steering itself. There was no better feeling than being locked in that narrow groove just off the breeze, riding one puff to the next, connecting the dots to keep myself flying. I chased that high across Lake Wequaquet until I lost the daylight, or my mother called me in.

It had been my father's idea that I should learn to sail. His passion for the ocean came to him later in his life, and it still burned with the intensity of a new and unlikely love. He'd grown up in a dirt-floor house in the arid, land-locked northern plains of Mexico. His Mexican father, an engineer working in a smelting and refining plant, met his mother, a New Englander and Smith College grad, when she went to Chihuahua to teach English in an American school—and, according to family lore, he'd serenaded her under her balcony with a mariachi band. My dad never saw a body of water bigger than a bath-tub, he liked to tell us, until the first time he saw a swimming pool at a country club—and he was dazzled.

After my grandfather died of tuberculosis, my grandmother moved my father, who was fourteen at the time, and his three much younger siblings to Worcester, Massachusetts, where she became head-mistress of a local school. After graduating from Williams College, my father went to Tulane Medical School in New Orleans. He got hooked on sailing on Lake Pontchartrain, the forty-mile-wide estuary on the city's northern border. To improve his navigation skills, he took a US Power Squadrons course that happened to use charts of the waters surrounding Cape Cod, and that bent arm–shaped peninsula that jutted into the waters of the northern Atlantic seemed magical to him. When he was recruited to set up an ear, nose, and throat medical practice in Hyannis, a town of about ten thousand people midway up the Cape's southern shore, he jumped at it. He married, had a daugh-ter, Ann, and then got divorced. He met my mother, Susan, a Jewish divorcee who had briefly stepped away from her teaching and publish-ing career to work in a local needlepoint shop, at a cocktail party. They began dating shortly after she came into his clinic for an appointment.

My earliest memories are being with my family—my dad, my mother, Ann, and my younger sister, Jennifer—on my father's little sailboat, a twelve-foot Kingfisher with a Bermuda blue hull and white decks. We'd put it in near the mouth of the tidal Centerville River and sail into the open waters of Nantucket Sound. Then we'd anchor off a broad beach and wade ashore with a picnic lunch. Other days, we'd launch into Osterville's West Bay from a sandy ramp near the old Wianno Yacht Club and sail the quiet inland waters. I remember the smell of beach roses and Coppertone, and I remember the joy in my father's face as he navigated that little boat across the broad shallows fringed by marsh grasses and long stretches of white sand.

When conditions were right, we'd circumnavigate the private island occupied by the gated, residential Oyster Harbors Club. Bill Koch, the billionaire who would finance the winning America's Cup boat in 1992, owned a waterfront mansion there. More intriguing to me at the time was the story that Captain Kidd was said to have buried treasure on the west side's Noisy Point in the 1600s, and that the trove was guarded by a shrieking witch whose ghost still haunted the island.

When I was eight years old, my father signed me up for a summer learn-to-sail program at the Hyannis Yacht Club, where some of his friends were members. The white-clapboard clubhouse had a long, weathered dock jutting into Lewis Bay on the sandy shore between Hyannis's inner harbor and Nantucket Sound. Ferries bound for or returning from Nantucket and Martha's Vineyard islands went by all day, sounding their low horns as they churned through the deep-water channel directly in front of the club.

I hated camp on the first day. Partly, it was the miserable June weather, cold and damp and gray. But I went back, and somehow, the second session felt like the best day of my life. I had learned how to rig a Beetle Cat, the wide-beamed, twelve-foot wooden dinghies modeled after nineteenth-century whaleboats that the club used for its kids' program. That single accomplishment changed me forever. Here was a thing I could do on my own. I couldn't wait to go back.

The instructors presented an award every Friday to the sailor of the week. To win, you had to show up on time, be responsible, have a positive attitude, and be meticulous about taking care of your boat. I was determined to earn that prize—a construction paper cut-out of a Beetle Cat—every week. When the program ended, I had amassed a pile of them.

By the next summer, I was racing. In retrospect, it was too much, too soon. I hadn't had enough time in a boat to begin to understand even the most basic principles of wind and tide and current. Not fully grasping the *why* of sailing would dog me throughout my competitive career. Well into my late teens, I raced with a little kid's glee and an innate feel for boat handling. Glee and feel are good, but they can get you only so far.

Sailing is essentially a physics experiment on water; every time you launch, you are trying to generate optimal forward movement by balancing above-water and under-water forces. My not grasping the *why*, the science of it, beyond the most fundamental levels put me at a disadvantage on the racecourse, especially as I moved up the ranks. I never asked enough questions. Not that I wasn't curious—I was. But my shyness kept me from speaking up, and as the years went by, it got harder and harder for me to admit what I didn't know.

In the fall of 1988, my father bought a 1922 Beetle Cat. It had been clumsily restored, and my father wanted to bring it back to its original glory and make it a faster, lighter boat. He moved our two cars out of the garage and set up the hull on wooden cradles. The only heat was from our clothes dryer's exhaust, and most of that rose straight to the ceiling, but I loved working out there on the boat next to my dad. Those winter weekends were the only chance I had to be with him for any length of time. He was a busy doctor, always on call, working long hours during the week.

By then, he had become a world-famous expert in diving and hyperbaric medicine, a field he'd become interested in after treating local lobstermen who had diving-related illnesses. He was in demand as a speaker at conferences all over the world. He taught diving medicine to physicians and ran hyperbaric chambers to treat scuba divers with decompression sickness. I thought he was a super-hero, even while I resented him for being gone so often. Why was he off saving people in other families and not spending time with ours? Admittedly, his renown did bring some perks to my family; we sometimes got to trail along with him to tropical dive resorts. I did my first open-water dive at age eight and became a certified scuba diver at twelve.

My father had no experience with wooden boat building or repair, so we made regular pilgrimages to Howard Boats in Barnstable and Concordia Yachts in New Bedford, both boatyards that built and repaired Beetle Cats, to ask for advice and buy authentic parts. The shops were filled with a dazzling array of tools and boats in various stages of construction. Fine sawdust and fragrant curls of shaved cedar covered their floors. I listened as the in-house boat builders explained to my dad how to replace caulking, lay planks edge to edge to follow the hull's curve, and bend wood using wet towels and a household iron. I remember being amazed that there were things my father didn't know how to do—and that he didn't seem to be at all self-conscious about asking for help.

It took us two winters to finish the Beetle Cat. When spring came, we trailered the boat, now sporting a fresh coat of forest green topside paint, to the yacht club, which by then we had joined. Now we had to start the process of making it watertight.

Wooden boats tend to dry out over the winter, and as they do, their bottom planks shrink, leaving gaps wide enough for water to seep through. The way to combat this is to swell those boards until they squeeze the caulking tight enough to create a seal. This means allowing the boat to take on water, again and again, until the spaces close up. Shivering alongside other wooden boat owners who were doing the same thing, we eased the Beetle Cat into the shallows just off the beach, dropped an anchor off its stern, and tied its bowline to the dock. Then we watched as it started to fill with seawater. Every day for a week or so, my parents dropped me off after school so I could bail it out, until one day I arrived and it was dry. It was a marvel—that nearly sinking something could make it seaworthy.

I named that boat *Sea Fan*. I thought it was a clever play on words, giving a nod to the delicate soft coral I'd seen while diving in the Cayman Islands and to the fact that I was indeed a fan of the sea. My friends laughed at the name; they'd named their boats things like *Challenger* and *Rampage*. But I thought my name was perfect. And *Sea Fan* was no lightweight. In 1991, I won the Commodores' Cup, presented to the Beetle Cat club champion. I was ecstatic that my name would be engraved on that silver trophy below the names of some of my sailing heroes who had won it before me.

4

We'd had a fun, productive practice that afternoon. In the broad Redwood Creek basin, Clinton and I had set up mock races so the team could work on starts and on tactics to use if their boats were in the lead or coming from behind. I was happy to see that for those three hours, at least, everyone seemed to tap into some of the joy that had drawn us to our sport in the first place.

We hadn't had an easy fall. Some of the players were unhappy with the way I coached, and they'd been vocal about it. They questioned the drills I chose to run, the amount of input I gave them on the water, the way I picked starters for each regatta. I listened to their complaints and implemented some of their suggestions, but they still pushed back. They were angry that they weren't getting the results they wanted on race days, and they blamed me. I liked and respected them, but I also thought they just weren't as good as they thought they were—they didn't seem willing to put in the work to improve. I rewarded players who trained hard and didn't make excuses—even if they were newer to the team. The discord divided us. In our debrief meetings, I felt like I'd lost half the locker room.

Part of what made the friction painful for me was that I recognized myself in those unhappy players. In college, I hadn't put the effort in to understand how to get faster. I thought I was better than I was. And I understood the pain of seeing shiny new freshmen come in and steal your spotlight. It happened in every sport.

But that October afternoon, in bright sun, with low humidity and a steady breeze, I felt some hope. We'd had good results at the Pacific Coast Collegiate Sailing Conference Singlehanded Championships in Long Beach the previous weekend. Four of our players had qualified for nationals, which were coming up in early November in Galveston, Texas. Earlier that week, we'd had an emotional team meeting during which I acknowledged I should have made my expectations clearer. I said I expected commitment and hard work and good communication. For my part, I promised to be more transparent. I presented a plan to give regular updates about where everyone stood as we moved closer to nationals. Talking about it all seemed to help ease some of the tension, but I know the divide ran deep.

After the boats had been put away and the team and Clinton had taken off, I lingered for a few moments, listening to the easy slap of water against the dock and the metallic ping of halyards against masts. A great blue heron glided low over Bair Island, which was awash in honey-colored light. The slant of the sun, the crispness of the air, the smell of the saltmarsh—it all took me back to being a kid on Cape Cod after the tourists had left the place to us year-rounders. I was aware at that moment of how lucky I was to be in that place, doing the thing I loved most. I promised myself I'd work even harder to get the team to a better place.

JUST AS I PULLED ONTO THE freeway, my cell phone rang. Typically, I wouldn't have answered—it was prime robocall hour—but I saw that the caller was from Newport Beach, a big recruiting area. I expected to hear a high school sailor's voice when I picked up. Instead, it was a man who introduced himself as Rick Singer.

He said he was a college recruiter who had worked with several Stanford coaches. He was going to be on campus the next day and wondered whether we could meet to talk about sailing. He wanted to discuss how he might be able to help me out. I'd never gotten a call from a recruiter before, never even heard of a recruiter in our sport. I was curious enough to say I'd see him in the morning in my office.

Recruiting was always on my mind, but especially at that time of year. In the coming weeks, I'd be doing college night presentations and sailing clinics all over the country and meeting the next crop of high school juniors who were interested in Stanford. I'd also be scouting the big holiday regattas in Florida where top young prospects from all over the world would be competing.

Before the recruiting season got into full swing, though, I had to figure out who I was looking for. On a whiteboard in my office, I mapped everything out—who was graduating, what freshmen were coming in, what positions needed filling—and I carried a picture of that board on my phone so I could pull it up and study it when I was on the road. I reviewed it often to make sure I wasn't missing something.

Stanford University certainly wasn't a hard sell. About thirty minutes south of San Francisco, it had a gorgeous campus with grand sandstone buildings, walkways lined with palm trees, stellar sports facilities, and acres of gardens and green space. Palo Alto had a near-perfect climate year-round, which was a huge draw for kids who'd grown up sailing in the Northeast and Europe. Stanford's reputation as a feeder school for Silicon Valley made it particularly appealing to students who dreamed of cutting-edge tech careers.

On top of all that, it was the most selective college in the country. I had no trouble attracting some of the best young sailors in the world.

Lately, though, with all the tension on our team, I'd been thinking I didn't necessarily want to recruit only the very best. I was more interested in bringing in players who had a growth mindset, a concept I'd gotten excited about after reading *Mindset: The New Psychology of Success* by Stanford psychology professor Carol Dweck. The premise is that people with fixed mindsets believe they are who they are—that their abilities and talents are immutable. People with growth mindsets see themselves as works in progress and believe abilities can be developed. Those were the kids I wanted to coach.

Some years, I knew I was looking for strong singlehanded sailors who could do well for us in solo racing events. Other years, I focused on finding talented skippers and crews. Skippers did the crucial steering in doublehanded boats; crews handled front-of-the-boat duties. In some ways, crews were the most critical piece of the recruiting puzzle—and they were also the hardest to find. Ideally, they would be excellent athletes with the strength, agility, and endurance to get through the eighteen short-course races we typically had at weekend regattas. But they also had to be adept at managing the mental side of competition.

It is a fact of racing that when things get real "out there" for whatever reason—a blown start or a near-collision rounding a mark—skippers tend to take their frustrations out on their crew. Crews have to be unflappable even when their drivers lose it. Unfortunately, meltdowns happen more often than they should. At a regatta in Hawaii, I'd seen a helmsman—one of the best sailors in the country—scream "Fuck!" and break his carbon tiller extension in two. Good crews know how to talk drivers down—and get them to prepare, calmly, for the next race—in much the way top golf caddies get players to forget about that last triple bogey and move on to the next tee.

Whether they were skippers or crew, though, Stanford sailors also had to be willing to make a major commitment to the team. Our sport spanned two seasons and staged six national championships every year. In the fall, we competed in match racing—one boat with a crew of four going head-to-head against another in a round-robin format—and in men's and women's singlehanded racing. In the spring, we vied for three more national titles: coed and women's doublehanded, with one skipper and one crew per boat in a traditional mass start format; and team racing, an often wild round-robin event (I'd heard it compared to March Madness) in which three double-handed boats from one school went against three from another and tried to out-maneuver each other on a short, N-shaped course.

The biggest prize in collegiate sailing is the Leonard M. Fowle Trophy, presented to the team with the best overall record across both seasons. It had bounced back and forth between Yale, the College of Charleston, and Boston College for the previous decade. No team west of the Mississippi had ever won it. Every year, I told our players they could make history if they brought home the Fowle. It was a powerful carrot. Three times we finished less than one point behind the winners. Getting so close made me want to work that much harder to find the recruits who could pull it off. I wanted it for the team, and yes, I wanted it for me. I dreamed of being known as the coach who built Stanford sailing into the best in the country.

If anyone could help me get there, like maybe this Rick Singer guy who was coming to see me in the morning, I was open to hearing what that person had to say.

5

I had my usual at Jimmy V's Sports Café—one egg over easy, avocado, sausage, hash browns, and an English muffin—on the ground floor of the athletics building, officially the Arrillaga Family Sports Center. The building was named after John Arrillaga, a billionaire alum and one of the largest landowners in Silicon Valley, who had donated more than $200 million to the university over the years. His name was also on the gym, the alumni center, a dining hall—and the Stanford sailing and rowing center. He was a hands-on benefactor; I often saw him eating in the café.

I finished breakfast, walked upstairs, swiped my ID card, and entered the varsity sports suite where I had an office. Just a few minutes after I settled in at my desk, I was startled to see a man at my open door. Ordinarily, when I had visitors, I'd get a call from the receptionist, and I'd go down to greet them and bring them through security.

"John?" he said, smiling broadly. "Rick Singer."

I invited him in. Singer was wiry and fit-looking, with a close-cropped helmet of silver hair, a deep tan, and a narrow, lined face. His choice of clothing for a meeting—T-shirt, shorts, flip-flops, and a tennis visor—screamed Southern Cal to me. I felt overdressed in my button-down shirt and khakis. I invited him to sit at a small round table and joined him there.

Singer told me he ran a company that helped high school students get into elite colleges. Mostly he focused on academics, but he also worked with athletes, especially tennis and basketball players, as they navigated recruiting and admissions. He said his background as a coach gave him a leg up in that world; he understood the process and knew a lot of people. Now he was looking to expand into smaller sports.

"So, tell me about sailing," he said. He locked his hands behind his neck, stretched out his legs, and crossed them at the ankles.

I told him there were about two hundred college sailing teams in seven different conferences. Fifty or so had varsity status with full-time coaches, but most were club sports, run by students or volunteers. All the programs competed against each other. That was the main reason why the Inter-Collegiate Sailing Association (ICSA) had banned scholarships; they wanted to keep the playing field level.

"And we have no independent recruiters like you," I said. "I mean, the idea of sailors being recruited for college teams at all, that's pretty new."

Singer wanted to know how I evaluated prospects, who my chief competitors were, what my timeline was, where most of my sailors came from, how I spotted talent, how much support I got from admissions. He listened intently when I answered, interjecting "wow" and "really" as I spoke.

"How much help do you have?" he asked.

"I have an assistant coach, but I pretty much do all the recruiting."

"You good at it?"

"I think I am. We get really good kids. We lose some here and there to Harvard and Yale, but in the end, they're making decisions based on other factors, academics, location—so I can't control that."

"Sure. Outta your hands."

"What's hard is keeping a roster together for the long term. I have no problem recruiting A-plus players, but, and I know this might sound weird, I have too many. I mean, they can't all start, right? And if they aren't starting, and they have no assurance that they ever will, it's hard to keep them. And then they get annoyed. They hate sitting on the bench. They've never had to do that. For most of their lives, they just signed up for regattas and went."

Singer nodded. "Interesting."

"And they're so highly driven in other aspects of life, their classes and clubs and everything else, that they decide being a bench-sitter on the sailing team is not how they want to spend their time at Stanford. And I have no scholarships to hold them with."

"That's tough. No scholarships. So, you lose athletes."

"I can't blame them for moving on. But I need a full roster for practices. We're not on the Charles River like MIT or Harvard or Boston University. They've got boathouses so close they could throw rocks at each other. And then Tufts and Boston College go out and join them for practices. It's a huge advantage for them."

"And you gotta have a certain level of competition during practice," Singer said. "Same thing in basketball."

"Right. It makes it tough to improve."

Eventually, I mentioned that I'd been thinking about casting my recruiting net wider, trying to find strong athletes from other sports who might want to switch over to sailing.

"They'd be the kind of kids who'd show up every day and pick up the sport fast and be valuable as team players. I could teach them, but they'd already have that athleticism they could tap into. And they'd come to me without expectations or bad habits."

"Yeah, clean slate. I gotcha. Fantastic idea. You fit right in at Stanford, John," Singer said, flashing a smile. "Smart guy."

"I don't know about that," I said with a laugh.

"So you'd actually look at athletes from different sports?"

"Yes. Like gymnasts. I've had two walk on—one at Navy and one at Stanford—and they did amazingly well. Gymnasts are built for sailing. They have the balance, and the upper body and core strength."

"Really. Gymnasts. Wouldn't have guessed that."

"The Stanford girl walked on as a senior. She'd had enough of injuries, and she just couldn't do it anymore. But she was hypercompetitive and said, 'I can't go a year without playing a sport. You know, I've been doing it my whole life.' So, I said sure, love to have you. And I was shocked at how quickly she picked everything up. She ended up starting nationals for us her senior year."

"Wow. Very cool."

"And she was great for the team. She brought that discipline and commitment, you know, a real understanding of what it takes to be on a varsity sport. I learned a lot from her, too."

I glanced at my watch and was surprised to see that Singer and I had been talking for nearly two hours. I felt like I'd been shooting the breeze with a buddy over a couple of beers. And he seemed interested in everything I had to say. He was sympathetic when I told him I had a baby—my son, Nicholas, had been born eight months before—and that my constant traveling was tough on my wife. He was impressed by my team's recent successes, and he was rapt as I expounded on my coaching philosophy: *mindsets* and *team culture* and *blah, blah, blah.* God, I went on. My lawyer would tell me later Singer was exhibiting classic grooming behavior. The perpetrator picks his target, probes for soft spots, builds up trust. The abuse comes later.

"So, listen, before I go, I wanna tell you about this girl I have." He pulled in his legs and sat up straight. "She's from Hong Kong, goes to school in the UK. She says she's a good sailor. I don't know how good she is. Great grades. Can I send you her information? See if I'm in the right spot in thinking that somebody like you might want her?"

I said I was happy to take a look. I was familiar with Wellington College, her boarding school. A sophomore on my team had graduated from there.

He got up to leave. "Enjoyed talking to you," he said, extending his hand. "Can't wait to show you this recruit."

He paused in the doorway. "You know what? Why don't I have one of the coaches I've worked with here give you a call. He can vouch for me. Sound good?"

I said that would be fine.

I thought about Singer during my twenty-minute drive from campus to the boathouse. He seemed like a good guy, but he knew nothing about our sport. I doubted he could find players for me. On the other hand, it couldn't hurt to have another set of eyes out there, especially eyes I didn't have to pay for. I figured he'd bring me some bad people at first, but maybe, over time, he'd get better at it—and I wasn't out a thing by having him try.

After practice, I checked my phone and saw I had a voicemail. It was from Adam Cohen, a Stanford men's basketball assistant coach, whom I knew slightly. He had moved into my neighborhood the previous spring when he'd gotten the job.

He said he was calling about Rick Singer. "Just want you to know I've worked with Rick. He's a guy you can trust. Let me know if you want to talk about him some more."

It was reassuring to hear that from Adam. He surely had experience with working with recruiters like Singer. Plus, he was a fellow Stanford coach. At the time, I believed that we all looked out for each other and held ourselves to the highest standard.

By the time I got home, Singer had emailed me to say thank you and to let me know he'd be sending the Hong Kong sailor's transcript, scores, and sailing résumé. A few days later, the information arrived. The student's name was Yusi "Molly" Zhao. Singer was right about her grades; they were excellent. But her regatta results were just okay. Plus, she was a singlehanded sailor, and I'd already recruited one for next year. I didn't need this girl. She'd be welcome as a walk-on and could certainly be a practice player, but I wouldn't use an admissions slot for her. I emailed Singer to let him know I couldn't support her as a recruit.

He wrote back. "The family is pretty affluent. They're willing to donate a million dollars to your program if she gets in."

Holy shit. Was he serious? That kind of money would have a major impact on the team. At Stanford, as at most colleges, small, non-revenue-generating sports—in general, everything other than football and men's basketball—lived and died on donations. And as the head coach, I was responsible for bringing much of that money in. It hadn't always been that way. When I first arrived at Stanford in 2008, the athletic development office handled fund-raising. All the donations went into a central kitty called the Buck/Cardinal Fund and were then distributed to the school's thirty-six teams.

That model changed in 2012 when Bernard Muir replaced Bob Bowlsby as director of athletics. Muir, who had come to Stanford after stints as athletics director at Georgetown and the University of Delaware, expected coaches to solicit donations for their teams. That made me deeply uncomfortable. I'm no salesman; I hate asking for money. But I forced myself to take the lunch meetings and host the alumni dinners and make the pitches at parents' weekends. (I felt especially uneasy soliciting parents who were already forking over a couple hundred thousand dollars in tuition.)

The new athletics director also made it clear in my first meeting with him that the goal was to bring in endowments—gifts so substantial that their annual 5 percent yield could cover equipment, travel, and coaches' salaries in perpetuity. Muir's own position was endowed; officially, he was the Jaquish & Kenninger Director of Athletics, thanks to the largess of a charitable foundation established by two wealthy alumni.

Endowments hadn't always been the gold standard for athletics fund-raising. In fact, they were unheard of until 1982, when an investment banker named Roger Weiss gave Cornell University $750,000 to endow the head football coach position. Two years later, Princeton received an endowment from a group of alums for its men's basketball head coach; similar gifts for the Tigers' head football coach, and head men's track and field coach soon followed. Yale's first endowed athletics post came in 1988, when alum Joel Smilow, the chairman and CEO of Playtex, donated $1 million to fund the Bulldogs' football coach. Stanford received its first coaching endowment in 1989 from investment banker Brad Freeman, who gave $1.6 million to permanently attach his name to the Cardinal's director of football.

Endowments saved schools millions of dollars every year, and Stanford, out of necessity, seemed to be particularly good at hauling in those large gifts. As *The Wall Street Journal*'s Ben Cohen reported in 2013, "Stanford isn't like other football powers. It can't generate as much cash from its fans since it doesn't have nearly as many. Stanford Stadium seats about 50,000—half the size of some venues in the Southeastern and Big Ten conferences."

Cohen continued: "The normal revenues Stanford receives from football are so low, in fact, that its 36 varsity sports teams depend on something no other school has, or would dare rely so heavily on: an athletics-only endowment worth between $450 million and $500 million that pays out at 5.5% each year."

Cohen quoted Bernard Muir: "Many have looked at Stanford to say: 'How can we make that happen at our place?'"

One way schools were trying to make it happen was by actively encouraging endowments. Many published price lists, of sorts, on their websites, leaving no mystery as to how much money was required to attach your name (or the name of your choosing) to coaches of various sports. Want to cover a head coach at Harvard? According to gocrimson.com, a gift of $2 million would do it. Princeton's website suggested a $2.5 million gift for a head coach, $1 million for an assistant. Duke University let it be known that $5 million would endow the athletics director, the head football coach, or the head men's and women's basketball coaches; coaches of Blue Devils Olympic sports were yours for a mere $2 million.

So, that million-dollar donation Rick Singer was dangling? That could endow my assistant coach's salary and free up those funds to hire a second assistant. I could also use the money to buy boats—we had to replace a fleet of eighteen sailboats every five to eight years at the cost of about $120,000—and to purchase a replacement for one of our beat-up team SUVs. Plus, it could help pay for the more than a dozen trips a year we made to the East Coast for regattas, and for some of the programs I wanted to institute to address players' mental and physical health. On top of all that, I'd get another sailor on my roster.

I looked at Singer's email again to make sure I'd read it right. "They're willing to donate a million dollars to your program if she gets in. Is that something that you're interested in?"

I had no idea what Singer was setting into motion with these two lines, no idea that my life was about to take a devastating turn.

I considered my reply and then finally typed, "I don't know anything about that. But I'll ask the higher-ups."

6

I wasn't sure whether what Singer was suggesting—the possibility of a million-dollar donation if Molly Zhao enrolled in Stanford—was something that might influence admissions. I certainly knew some version of that went on and had been going on for decades. Families made significant contributions, got their names on buildings, or seats on powerful boards and committees, and—surprise!—their children were admitted to the school.

The often-cited poster boy for this apparent quid pro quo was Jared Kushner, Donald Trump's son-in-law. As author Daniel Golden wrote in *The Price of Admission*, not long before Jared—an average high school student with below Ivy League–standard test scores—was admitted to Harvard, his billionaire father, Charles, pledged $2.5 million to the school. Golden wrote that at least one former official at the Frisch School, Jared's high school in Paramus, New Jersey, expressed shock that young Kushner had gotten in when other students with better records had not.

A Stanford report to the California state legislature would later confirm what I'd suspected—that having the *potential* to donate was indeed mentioned in the files of some applicants. The Office of the Provost wrote that 16.2 percent of admitted Class of 2023 students were legacies (those whose parents had gone to Stanford as undergrads or grads) and acknowledged that some of their admission files "also noted a history of philanthropy." An additional 1.5 percent of the enrolling class "had no legacy affiliation with Stanford, but their admission files noted a history of philanthropy." Still, the report insisted, family connections and/or a track record of giving meant nothing "if an applicant to Stanford is not highly competitive academically."

I certainly had no experience with what Singer was offering on behalf of the Zhao family—and I'd received zero training from Stanford about the ethics or legality of donations. I was glad the university had an entire athletic development department dedicated to evaluating and processing gifts. My assumption, mistaken I now know, was that any major contribution would trigger a thorough investigation.

I called one of the decision makers in the development office. "So, here's the situation. I have a girl who I'm not going to support, but I'd be happy to have her as a walk-on. And I've just been told that if she gets in, her family would like to donate $1 million to the sailing program."

"Really. Wow," she said.

"I know. So, what I'm wondering is, does the potential to donate have an impact on admissions? Is that a thing? Or would athletics maybe have another spot I could use on her?"

"I don't know. But let me look into it."

A few days later, I received an email from Adam Cohen. He said he was touching base with me about the recruit Rick Singer had mentioned. It struck me as odd that Singer would have bothered to share specifics about Molly Zhao with Cohen, a basketball coach. I wrote back to say I was waiting to hear from development about options.

Later that week, my contact in the development office called me. "You know what? The school does do something like that. But I was told a million dollars isn't enough to have an impact on the application."

"Really? They said that? A million isn't enough?"

"They did," she said.

"Wow."

"Do you think the family might be willing to donate more?"

I told her I had no idea. I was glad she didn't press me to go back to Singer and ask.

About a week later I received an email from another contact in the development office, Heather Owen, the senior associate athletics director. It was cc'd to Beth Goode, the executive associate athletics director, who also served as a liaison to Stanford's undergraduate admissions office.

"Here's the scoop," Heather wrote. "We have placed a request for an additional admissions slot for sailing on the list that Beth manages (as you can imagine, a number of requests similar to this come in each year). Bernard and Beth meet, discuss, and determine those sports that will receive additional admissions slots each year. This decision is largely based on the number of admissions slots that are not used. I will place Molly on the development 'watch list' to indicate to admissions that development has an interest in the ultimate admissions decision."

I'd never heard of a development watch list, but I wasn't surprised to hear that such a thing existed. It was out of my hands now. Plus, I was about to leave on a two-week recruiting trip and I had to get organized.

When I returned and there was no further update from the development office about Molly Zhao, I figured the whole thing was a dud. My brief fantasy of what the team might do with a million dollars evaporated as easily as it had arrived. I had had the feeling it was too good to be true, anyway.

I emailed Singer to let him know that nothing had changed, and there didn't seem to be a slot for Molly, even going through other channels. He asked if the two of us could meet with Heather together to press his client's case. I said no. Heather already had all the pertinent information, and there was no further discussion needed, as far as I was concerned. I trusted her assessment. Besides, I felt like bringing Heather into the conversation would reflect poorly on me. I didn't want her to think I couldn't handle my own business. Looking back on it now, I wonder whether Singer thought he might be able to pull Heather into his scheme if he'd gotten an audience with her.

Just before the spring 2017 season got under way, I attended an all-coaches meeting, one of a monthly series that featured various speakers from Stanford teams. At this one, David Shaw, the head football coach, or rather the Bradford M. Freeman Director of Football, addressed the group about his recruiting philosophy. He said he had passed on a top quarterback because he "wasn't a Stanford man" but had happily brought on a lesser player who he believed would be a better fit. Hearing that from Coach Shaw, whose team had gone 10–3, won a bowl game, and been ranked twelfth overall nationwide that past season, strengthened my resolve to focus more on personality and values and less on stats as I recruited my next class.

Team culture was very much on my mind that spring. The team's internal troubles had not disappeared over winter break. Clinton and I had tried to address the squad's concerns, but we couldn't mend the rift that had developed between the two factions—one that supported what we were doing and one that fought us. It was frustrating for everyone. Somehow, we were still sailing well. In April, we won all three Pacific Coast Collegiate Sailing Conference championships, and at nationals in Charleston in May, we were in the hunt for a podium spot in women's doublehanded going into the final two races—and ended up fifth. We finished seventh in team racing and made it to the coed finals, but faltered after a great first day.

With the season coming to a close, the athletics department distributed its annual end-of-year survey to players, sent out in part to help determine whether a coach deserved to keep his or her job. In past years, I'd received almost no feedback about the surveys, other than an informal "Keep up the good work" from the athletics director in charge of sailing. But in mid-June, after the 2016–2017 reviews were turned in, I was summoned to a meeting with Bernard Muir.

I was nervous when I walked into Bernard's corner office and found both him and Heather Owen standing near a round table waiting for me. I was used to being dwarfed by them; both had been college basketball stars in the 1990s: Heather was six-feet-four and had played for Stanford; Bernard was six-feet-six and had played at Brown. It just added to the anxiety. Bernard asked me to sit, and I took a chair facing a wall hung with framed color photos of Stanford teams.

"We need you to explain what's going on with this survey," Bernard said.

"Sorry, I'm not sure what you're talking about," I said.

"The comments we got back." Bernard read from a paper he had in front of him. "'You're not friendly to foreigners. You're not transparent about who is starting. You swear. The team isn't as competitive as it should be.'"

"I don't agree with any of that," I said, feeling my face flush. I could guess who had written the comments—the players who were angry at me for not running the team the way they thought best. "But I haven't seen the surveys, so it's hard for me to respond right now. Can I read them?"

After some discussion, Bernard said Heather could send them to me with those comments redacted that would make it obvious which players had written them.

"Team culture is paramount," Bernard said.

That sounded good, and I certainly wanted to foster a positive, fun, and supportive environment. But the fact was that Bernard cared deeply about winning. Evidence of that was in a trophy case on the first floor of the athletics building. For twenty-four straight years, Stanford had won the Directors' Cup, a globe-shaped Waterford crystal trophy presented to the school with the nation's best overall record across all sports. Although the sailing program's successes didn't count toward the award because we were not under the NCAA umbrella, I understood that I was expected to achieve that level of success. Our coaching bonuses, after all, were based on championships won—not on the happiness of the players.

"Yes," I said. "I'll definitely work on that. Team culture is really important to me, too."

"And what's this about not being competitive?" Bernard asked. "Why aren't you getting good results?"

"Actually, we've done quite well."

"Really? What have you done?"

"We've won conference champ—"

Bernard lifted his hand to stop me. "Next year's survey better improve or there will be an issue."

A FEW DAYS AFTER HEATHER SENT me the surveys, I responded. I promised to work on communication and to institute programs aimed at improving team culture. I vehemently denied being unfriendly to foreigners; that was simply baseless. Did I swear? Yes, occasionally, to get my team's attention. I also compiled a list of all of the team's successes—every conference victory, every national championship appearance—since I'd taken over as head coach. I was humiliated by the whole exercise—the idea that I had to prove myself after more than a decade there. I emailed my lengthy defense. Bernard never responded.

Molly and I started gearing up for a busy summer. I had several Club 420 regattas to oversee in the United States and Canada, and I was also doing kids' racing clinics all over the country. Plus, I would be firming up my next recruiting class. Molly had an equally hectic schedule running summer programs for PYSF. She was also in charge of US Sailing development team camps, and she was, of course, taking care of Nicholas alone when I was on the road. On top of all of that, she was pregnant again.

The weeks rolled by, and suddenly it was late August and I was back in my office getting ready for the start of the fall semester. I was always a little nervous waiting for the students to arrive. These were kids with perfect SAT scores, extraordinary résumés, exceptional minds. I was never going to be the smartest guy in the room with this group. They challenged me. Mostly, that was a good thing—I learned a lot from them—but it could also be intimidating. On top of my usual unease, I was anxious about how team dynamics were going to play out. And now I knew I was being watched by Bernard. I was worried about being fired. I needed to have a winning, drama-free season.

One day I was just packing up to go home when my phone rang. The caller ID said Rick Singer.

"Hey, Rick," I said.

His reply was garbled. It was a bad connection, which was something I was used to dealing with in the athletics building where the cell service was notoriously awful. It had become routine to answer a call and then quickly leave my office and make my way outside to a broad alley between the tennis stadium and our building where reception was much better. All the coaches in the building did it. It was a running joke; here was Stanford, this incubator of high-tech geniuses, and the school couldn't figure out how to make cell phones work. (A 2016 New York Times article about this paradox noted that

Steve Jobs himself had to stand outside his Palo Alto home, just a few blocks from campus, to make a call.)

The problem with making the trek to better cell service was that it took a few minutes to get there. From my office, I had to go down a long hallway, through some double doors, down two flights of stairs, past the equipment room, and then through another set of doors to the exit. The service actually deteriorated as you walked, and about half the time, the calls were dropped. Sure enough, I lost Singer as I descended into the stairwell.

I called him back when I got outside.

"Sorry about that," I said.

"No worries. I just wanna to tell you how excited Molly is about getting into Stanford. Thanks for all your help."

That Molly Zhao had been admitted to Stanford was news to me. I hadn't supported her. I'd never even brought her up with admissions.

"I didn't do anything, but—"

"No, no, you were amazing."

"I didn't—"

"You were terrific," he said. "But the family is disappointed they didn't hear early, ya know? They were hoping for that, like a little heads-up. So, they were kinda miffed."

"Well, that's good she got in on her own. Do you think she's going to sail?"

"You know, I think she's gonna focus on academics at first. See how things go."

"Sure. That's understandable."

I'd encountered plenty of kids who thought they wanted to be on a college team until they faced the reality of trying to juggle a varsity sport with classwork. I'd even known recruited athletes to quit before they made it to a single practice. No rule required kids to sail on the team—even if I'd used one of my admissions slots on them.

"But, hey, I convinced the family they should still donate to your program," Singer said.

"Really? Why would they?"

"I tried for the full million. Not gonna happen. They wanted that early decision. So, they're going to do $500,000 to Stanford. Sound good?"

"Wow. Uh, yes. God, that would be amazing."

Had I heard that right? Their daughter didn't plan to sail, but they still wanted to donate half a million dollars to the team? This whole thing was baffling.

"And so, look, with this donation, I have to do it through my foundation, okay?"

"Okay, I think that's fine," I said. "I'll ask development."

I was pumped. This would be the largest donation I'd ever brought in. The gift that was a very close second had been almost as mystifying. About a year earlier, I'd received a call at 6 a.m. from a man whose daughter was on the Stanford equestrian team. He said he was a sailor and wanted to donate to the sailing program. He asked me what I needed in terms of equipment and support. Two days later, a $495,000 check arrived in my mailbox. I found out later he'd also paid for a practice range for the golf team. People with buckets of money—and there were tons of them in Silicon Valley— sometimes did odd, but wonderful, things.

After Singer hung up, I walked downstairs to development to tell Heather the great news.

"That's fantastic. Congrats!" she said. "And you didn't do anything for this?"

"No, nothing," I said. "I never took her information to admissions. Nothing."

"Incredible. You're making my job easy for me."

"One thing. Rick Singer asked if he could donate through his foundation. Is that a problem?"

"No, that should be fine," Heather said. "We just need to figure out how to steer it."

I suggested the money go to buy equipment, and Heather agreed. She told me to ask Singer to make out the check to Stanford and to write "sailing equipment fund" on the memo line. She also said I should ask him to write a brief letter specifying that the money was to be used at the sailing coach's discretion.

By the end of the week, I had a $500,000 check from Singer's Key Worldwide Foundation. I put the check in the top drawer of my desk until Singer's letter arrived. Then, with the paperwork in place, I took the envelope with the check in it downstairs to development.

Bernard Muir happened to be coming out of a meeting in a nearby conference room. Heather called him over.

"We have to congratulate John," she said. "He just brought us that check for $500,000."

"Oh, hey, great job," he said, reaching out to shake my hand. "You must be excited about this."

"Thanks. I am."

"And you didn't do anything for it, right?"

"No, nothing. This is a donation from a Chinese family through Rick Singer. He's a college—"

"Oh, we know Rick," Bernard said, waving his hand to cut me off. He looked over at Heather. "We know Rick well."

7

A few weeks after I turned that first check over to development, Singer emailed me about another prospect named Bodhi Patel. He said he was a terrific student, really driven, and that he came from a wonderful family, whom Singer happened to know well.

"Maybe not the best sailor, but he's the type of kid that we've talked about. He can help you out, fill your roster," he wrote. "I'll send you his info."

Bodhi's regatta results were mediocre, but he did sail on his Bay Area high school team, which was a point in his favor. In a sport as individual as sailing, youth sailors often worked their way through the ranks on their own. When they were thrown into the unfamiliar structure of a college team, they sometimes struggled. Bodhi's academics were very good, maybe good enough for Stanford, but I already had other prospects in mind for my last admissions slot—and they were all better sailors.

Singer texted me almost daily about Bodhi. "You should support him." "He'd be great for your team." "Do it." It started to get annoying. Then one day, he emailed to say that Bodhi had decided to apply early to the University of Pennsylvania. I wished him luck. I was glad to be done with it.

I didn't hear from Singer again until January 13, 2018. He called when I was walking through the Salt Lake City airport, heading home from the midwinter ICSA college coaches meeting in Park City. I couldn't wait to get back. Molly's due date was just two weeks away.

"Hey, so listen," he said. "Bodhi got deferred from UPenn. He's really bummed."

"That's too bad." I was moving fast, shouldering my backpack, pulling my carry-on, and dodging people on the way to my gate.

"He wants to know if there's a possibility you'd support him through regular decision."

Announcements were coming over the loudspeaker.

"Sorry, what?"

"Would you support him if he applies regular decision?"

"Regular decision? I don't know. Maybe. Let me take a look."

Over the next few weeks, Singer peppered me with texts about his client. "Super hard worker." "Fantastic kid." "You should do it."

I didn't pay much attention to his messages because I had more important things on my mind. Nora O'Bryan Vandemoer was born on January 26. She was perfect. Molly and I were over the moon.

Eventually, I got around to telling Singer that I was sorry but I didn't think I could support Bodhi as a recruit. And besides, I said, if UPenn had deferred him, it seemed unlikely that he had the academics to get into Stanford.

Singer was undeterred. The texts kept coming. One day, there was this one: "The family is very affluent. I'm sure they would help your program if he gets in."

"That's great," I wrote back. "But we'll just have to see what admissions says."

He said he wanted to talk to my athletics director to see what we could do to help Bodhi. I said no. More texts followed. I wanted him to back off, but he had facilitated the sailing program's largest donation, so I knew I had to tread lightly. I'd learned over my years of coaching and fund-raising that most donors expect things in return for their gifts. They want access. Inside scoop. VIP passes. Tickets to big games. They want my ear. So when they called, no matter what time of day it was, they expected me to answer. And I felt like I had to talk to them—they'd given so much, the least I could do was take their calls. Usually, they just wanted to chat, find out how the team was looking, who I had in the recruitment pipeline, what I thought about our chances at nationals.

Parents who gave lavishly sometimes misconstrued their financial support as a guarantee that their child would get preferential treatment. One family had been extremely generous, but when I didn't start their son at nationals, they cut off all communication with me. They also told Patrick Dunkley, my program's athletics director at the time, that they would no longer be donating—at least not while I was still coach. They said I was hurting the program. Just a few weeks before, they'd acted like we were the best of friends.

Over time, I'd developed a default behavior with donors. I wasn't proud of it, but I saw it as self-preservation. When they called, I was exceedingly pleasant. I assured them I could get them whatever they were asking for. I said "yes," "of course," "fantastic," "thank you." But I wasn't listening. It pains me to say this. As a coach, I had always preached to my players that listening is essential. But I didn't take my own advice. If I'd had a proper conversation, paid attention, really listened to what Rick Singer was saying, I wouldn't have gotten into the monumental mess I was about to get into.

Over the years, I had talked with some of my fellow coaches about how they dealt with time-sucking donors, and they all said they did the same thing. Maybe there were better ways to deal with significant contributors, but I sure didn't know what they were—and Stanford had never offered any guidance. We were all fending for ourselves, kowtowing to our benefactors, who we so desperately needed so we could get back to coaching.

With Singer, I felt I was on even shakier ground. Not only had he brought in this huge gift from the Zhao family, which freed me up from having to do the nickel-and-dime fund-raising that I found so awkward, but he was also out there trying to find athletes for me. I needed to fill every one of my admissions slots. If I didn't use them all, I thought it very likely that Stanford would reduce my allotment the following year. Singer could be irritating, for sure, but he was connected to the two things I most needed to do my job well: athletes and the funding to help them compete. I believed it was in my team's best interest to keep him engaged.

Eventually, I told Singer I'd put Bodhi on the "list."

"He's on the list?"

"Yup," I said.

"Awesome."

I lied. There was no magic list. I didn't intend to take Bodhi's academic information to admissions. I just said that so Singer would stop bugging me about Bodhi, and for a while, it worked.

Just after regular admission decisions went out in April, Singer's name popped up on my caller ID.

"Bodhi didn't get in," he said when I picked up. "He's really disappointed."

I said I was sorry to hear that.

"But he's thinking of taking a gap year. Think you'd support him if he finishes off senior year strong? He's such an amazing kid and he really wants to work on his sailing. Maybe go to some summer camps."

I couldn't believe he was still going with this. What was the at-traction? Was I missing something? Singer's persistence was starting to make me second-guess myself. I'd dismissed Bodhi from the start. I hadn't even met him, although not for lack of trying. I'd asked Singer a few times to set up a meeting with his client. He promised he would make it happen but never followed through. Still, Singer had years of experience with spotting quality student-athletes. That was his busi-ness. Maybe I was making a mistake in not looking harder at Bodhi.

I pulled up his résumé and transcript on my phone. Yes, his regatta results weren't great. But Singer said Bodhi was serious about wanting to improve and about sailing for Stanford. Maybe he was someone I could work with. It could be that he just hadn't had the right coaching. One thing was certain: Bodhi needed me more than I needed him, and that in itself was appealing. The super-talented prospects I pursued were almost always kids who didn't need me as much as I needed them. They were going to get offers from every top school—and I'd learned that those in-demand kids weren't necessar-ily the best for team culture. Maybe it wouldn't be the worst thing to have a player who was not outstanding but was hungry for a chance and would feel he owed me for giving it to him.

I told Singer to send me Bodhi's grades after senior year ended. I warned him it was a long shot—after all, the kid had already been rejected by Stanford once. But if he took challenging classes, really ramped things up, there might be a chance. I knew Stanford loved to see tough workloads and upward trajectories with grades, but admis-sions worked in such mysterious ways, I had no clue how they might react to this unusual situation. I was curious to find out what they would say in a second go-round.

I had another reason for wondering how admissions would view Bodhi's repeat application. I had my eye on a high school senior, an outstanding singlehanded sailor, who was in a similar situation. Although I would have loved to have her on the team, she had contacted me too late in her junior year for me to support her. She'd applied to Stanford on her own and been rejected. A New England university had accepted her, but the financial aid offered was not what her family hoped for. Her parents had floated the idea with me that she turn down the other school and reapply to Stanford, this time as one of my top recruits. It would be a risk on her part, and I had no idea whether it would work. But if admissions offered Bodhi a pink envelope, it would show me they were at least open to students who reapplied, and I could feel more confident about recommending she do the same.

I was in the boathouse one afternoon when Singer called to ask whether he could stop by my office on campus the next day. I said that was fine. Once again, he appeared at my door—in shorts, T-shirt, sneakers, and a visor—without my first getting a call from the front desk. I never did figure out how he managed that. Was he so well-known to the athletics department that they just waved him through, or had he visited other coaches in the building before he came to see me?

We sat at the round table. Singer told me he was in the area running prospect ID camps—private fitness-, agility-, and skills-testing events staged to gather data about high school athletes that could then be disseminated to college coaches. The showcases, modeled after the National Football League's combines, had been around for a long time in college football and basketball but were becoming more common in other sports as kids—and their parents—searched for ways to get noticed by coaches. Even water polo and golf had combines.

"We so need that in sailing," I said. "I've been looking into it."

I told him I was on an ICSA committee tasked with researching what it would take to create standardized tests for high school–age sailors and an online clearinghouse to share the results. I said I was hoping US Sailing might get behind it.

"I've been thinking about expanding my camps into other sports," Singer said. "I wonder if I could get involved in that somehow. Maybe help bring the concept to sailing."

It seemed like a great fit. If US Sailing went forward with it, the organization would need a third party to run the camps and administer the fitness tests. Singer had experience doing exactly that. We talked for an hour or so about what it might look like, what kind of information would be valuable to coaches, how we might shoot and post video, what types of tests would be useful in evaluating a prospective sailing recruit. The more we talked, the more excited I got, and Singer obviously shared my enthusiasm.

"Listen," Singer said. "You know what? I'm thinking I could fund this myself."

"Really? Wow, that would be amazing."

"I wanna sit down with the president of the ICSA, you, me, him, and figure it out, all right? Come up with a plan to do this."

I said I'd love that.

"This is gonna be great, man!" he said, slapping his left hand on the edge of the table and smiling broadly. "Let's make it happen."

Then he leaned forward, clasped his hands, and looked me in the eyes. "Now, John, I wanna know. What can I do for you right now? What do you need?"

"Need? Like, for my team?"

"Yeah. Boats? Whad'ya need? Sails? I dunno. Tell me."

"What I need most is a second assistant coach. A woman. Three-quarters of my team is female, and I know they'd benefit from a female coach. We had one a few years ago, but I didn't have the funding to keep her."

"Gotcha."

"And we could really use a boatwright like rowing has—someone to maintain the equipment so I can just focus on the program."

Singer nodded. "How much would you need to do those things?"

"Money?" I asked.

"Yeah."

I calculated the salaries for each position.

"I guess it would be a total of around $110,000," I said.

"Uh-huh."

We sat in silence for a moment.

"Look, I love what you're doing here," Singer said. "Love your program, everything. I wanna be more involved. So, I'm gonna take a risk, all right? Take a risk on you, because I believe in you. I'm gonna give you the $110,000. No strings attached."

"That would be incredible!" I said. "Wow, thank you."

"Just to show you my support. Hopefully, I bring you good recruits, you're excited about them, and it's a, it's a, fruitful relationship in the end. But no strings, all right? No strings. We'll get you that $110,000. Done. I'll have my accountant send you a check."

I was elated. This guy, who knew his stuff, had so much confidence in me that he was willing to hand over ridiculous amounts of money to my program on a whim. I was starting to feel like I was the coach of the year. He loved my program. *My* program. I'd never before thought of a team I coached as *my* program. Not at Stanford or the US Naval Academy or St. Mary's. I'd felt responsibility and love for the teams, yes, but I always thought of them as the players' programs. The athletes were what mattered. But now I was being told that *I* mattered, and I lapped it up.

I cringe now at the thought of how jacked up I was by Singer's flattery. To look back and know he was just playing me, to see what an easy mark I had been—it makes me ill.

After Singer left, I trotted downstairs to tell Heather that Singer had offered me enough money to fund two staff positions. She congratulated me and said he should write "coaches' salaries" in the check's memo line. The envelope with the return address of the Edge College & Career Network arrived a few days later. I strutted it down to development.

8

Singer emailed me Bodhi's final high school grades in June 2018. They were excellent. He also attached Bodhi's sailing résumé, but since I'd already seen it several times, I didn't open it. I would regret that later when I was in a room full of lawyers. I decided to forward Bodhi's paperwork to admissions, and in a day or two, they got back to me with an offer of a pink envelope. I wasn't sure I'd end up using a slot on Bodhi, but at least I had him as a possible backup. More important, I now knew that the admissions department was open to giving pink envelopes to student-athletes it had previously rejected, and that seemed promising for the singlehanded sailor I really wanted. I let Singer know I'd be sending the pink envelope to Bodhi. He sounded delighted.

Molly and I were both gearing up for another hectic summer. We each had sailing camps to run, and I had a full calendar of Club 420 events. In late June, I headed to the first one—the Club 420 New England Championship in Stonington, Connecticut. It was a suffocating, humid ninety degrees when I arrived at the Wadawanuck Yacht Club. Out on the glassed-over Fishers Island Sound, the race committee boat I was on bobbed near the becalmed fleet waiting for even the feeblest breeze. We started and abandoned several races and then finally gave up and sent everyone in for the day. I was fried by the time I got back to my hotel room. I cranked up the AC, flung myself on the bed, and called Molly. Just after we hung up, my phone vibrated with a new text. Rick Singer.

"Just giving you a heads-up," he wrote. "Bodhi decided he doesn't want to sail on the team. He wants to be the team manager."

What the . . . ? Was he serious? After all this? I didn't recruit managers—we didn't even *have* a manager. I didn't have the energy to respond. I put the phone on the bedside table and fell asleep.

On the flight home, I actually gave some thought to recruiting Bodhi to manage the team. Maybe it wasn't the craziest idea. We'd begun using drones to film races and practices. I knew Dartmouth sailing had hired work-study kids to fly its drones. Stanford didn't have any student employment programs like that. Maybe I could teach Bodhi how to handle a drone and also have him sail as a practice player on some days. I stared out the window at the hazy grid of farmland far below me. Jesus, no, that was crazy. What was I thinking? Recruit a manager? Just to please Rick Singer? No way. I thought about how to respond and decided it was best not to answer at all. Maybe he'd get the message. I pulled the window shade down and closed my eyes.

A month or so later, Molly and I were sitting at a kids' hair salon at a low-rise outdoor shopping center about a block from the Stanford football stadium. Nicholas was getting a haircut. My phone buzzed with a text from Singer: "Can I call you?"

I told Molly I'd be right back and stepped outside to take the call.

"Got some bad news," Singer said.

"Okay."

I started walking along the storefronts in the shade of an overhang.

"Bodhi got off the waiting list for Brown, and he wants to do that."

"Wait, sorry, what?" I said, cutting across the parking lot to a small sitting area with benches under a lone palm tree. "Did you say Brown?"

Singer had never mentioned that Bodhi had an interest in Brown.

"Yeah. The family is super excited—and it's cheaper for them," he said with a laugh. "I just feel so bad this didn't work out, man."

"Okay, well, no problem. Brown's a great school."

Even though I was annoyed, I'd learned over the years never to be anything but upbeat about a student's choice. These were professional relationships between the prospect and the coach, or in this case, the college counselor and the coach. It was natural to be disappointed or even angry after you'd invested time pursuing a recruit. But I kept those feelings to myself. The sailing community was small; if you behaved like a jerk, word would travel among high school coaches, and potential recruits and their friends. In Bodhi's case, I didn't care all that much that he was stiffing me. In fact, I was relieved. I didn't have to think about him anymore.

"Yeah, he's happy. But, listen, I have three other kids I wanna run by you," Singer said.

"Okay . . ." I said. I was not wholly enamored of Rick Singer at this point. "But I've only got one spot left."

The first two students he described didn't sound great. But the third one got my interest.

"She's a gymnast. Super athletc, does some other sports. From Las Vegas, but her family has a place in Newport Beach. That's where she sails," Singer said.

This was exactly the kind of kid I was hoping to find. Gymnastics. Athletic. Sailing experience. It was as if she had been conjured up just for me. I would find out later that that was precisely the case.

After we hung up, I wondered what Singer meant about it being cheaper for Bodhi to go to Brown. The tuition had to be about the same at both schools. It seemed like a strange thing to say.

Over the next few weeks, Singer and I texted back and forth about Mia D'Angelo, the Las Vegas gymnast. He told me her family had a membership at the Newport Harbor Yacht Club and that she was also sailing at the US Sailing Center in Long Beach. She hadn't done any racing yet but was serious about improving and intent on using the summer to transition from gymnastics to sailing.

That wasn't unusual. I'd known plenty of kids who wanted to go to a Division 1 school but weren't skilled enough in their high school sport to compete at that level. They'd successfully transferred that love of team and competition to a college sport, like sailing and rowing, that welcomed walk-ons.

I was in Hyannis with my family when Singer emailed me Mia's transcript. She had excellent grades, but since I knew nothing about her high school, I couldn't predict how admissions would react. Sometimes, I'd show them straight A's, and they'd tell me that wasn't good enough. Other times, I'd see B's and think this kid doesn't have a chance, and they would say, "Looks great." It was all about the classes they were taking, the strength of their academic load. I'd learned not to get too excited about a prospect—even ones with 4.0's—before I got that first read.

I forwarded her information and was surprised to see a reply pop up from admissions just a few hours later. It usually took at least a few days to hear back.

"We can offer you a pink envelope for her."

Who was this girl? I searched her name and found a Wikipedia entry about a man I assumed to be her father. He was a billionaire casino owner and sports promoter—and a big-time philanthropist. I could only assume admissions had done the same basic research I was doing. I texted Singer to ask whether this was indeed Mia's dad.

"Yeah. You didn't know that name?"

"No," I wrote. "You think they might donate to the team?"

"I think this gentleman will really take care of the program."

"What kind of donation are we talking about? Could it be more than $500,000?"

"No, but there would probably be more later. If Mia is happy."

How had I gotten so damn lucky? Here was a girl who fit the exact profile of someone I'd been searching for, who also happened to be from a superwealthy family with a history of philanthropy who might very well make a large donation—maybe even an endowment—to my program. I knew she was an unusual recruit, and I'd have to make a case for her with admissions if I decided to use a slot on her. I'd do that later on an Athlete Ranking Form, the last piece of the recruitment package. As with all final recruits, I'd write a detailed defense of my choice, explaining how this particular person would help the team. That Mia's family had the means to make a significant donation seemed like something worth mentioning. It certainly couldn't hurt. After that, it was up to admissions to decide.

For now, though, I added Mia only to my Ranking and Justification form, which I would edit several times during the next eight weeks or so as prospects dropped off or were added. I put Mia at the bottom of the list and wrote, "She is an athlete from other sports who converted late to sailing. She has the potential to be a really athletic crew for us. She lives in Las Vegas during the year and commutes to Newport Beach to sail."

I believed all of that to be true. I could not have imagined that the FBI would be waving that very form under my nose at my kitchen table in about six months.

When I got back to Palo Alto, I picked up Mia's pink envelope from admissions and called Singer to ask for her mailing address. I also reminded him that I needed her complete athletics résumé. I wouldn't be able to move forward with her until I had that. The résumé wouldn't just tell me what other sports she had played but would also help me discern what kind of person she was. I liked to see captainships, state titles, MVP or Coaches awards—anything noteworthy that could help build the case that this recruit was not only an accomplished athlete, but a leader and an exemplary teammate as well.

"Yeah, I'll get that to you," Singer said. "Just send the application to me. I'm close to the family. I'm going to fly out and take it to them. Then I'm going to sit with Mia to help her fill it out. Make sure it's good."

I thought that was odd, but by now, I was used to Singer's quirks. In early September, my newly hired second assistant coach, Isabel (Belle) Strachan, arrived to start her job. I was thrilled to have her. She had just graduated from George Washington University, where she'd been a talented crew and led her team to its first three national championship appearances. She'd also coached in junior programs all over the country. I knew she would really help the team.

The school year got under way. I was happy to be launching with the team again, glad to smell the mudflats' dark funk and see the yellow hills of the eastern shore. Summer's strong thermal winds had yet to give way to autumn's lighter air. As I motored along with the sailors down Redwood Creek, I felt the breeze building. The full force of the wind hit us when we entered the open, white-cap–streaked bay. Sails snapped taut. Crews and skippers whooped as they committed to the hiking straps, legs fully extended, bodies stretched out nearly parallel to the water, spray blasting them in the face. I bounced along behind them and next to them, loving what I was seeing. I knew they were feeling it—the unmatchable, elemental joy of being fully powered in a small boat. There is nothing else like it. I remember thinking, *This is a good group. We're going to have a fantastic season.*

Even as I delighted in those first practices, I couldn't escape the stress I was feeling about my recruiting class for next year. Singer had yet to send me Mia's complete athletics information. He'd texted me a short list of sports she had played in high school, and I'd written back to tell him that wasn't good enough. I needed a detailed account of her sports background in traditional résumé form. I couldn't understand what was so hard about getting that to me.

Mia's incomplete application wasn't the only thing making me anxious. I was still waiting to hear from several other prospects about their plans. They had received pink envelopes during the summer, but I had no idea whether they would use them. And if they did submit their applications and Stanford admitted them, there was no guarantee that they would decide to enroll. These were mercurial seventeen- and eighteen-year-old sailors I was dealing with. I understood what they were going through. I'd been one of them.

9

At fourteen, I aged out of the Beetle Cat class and into Club 420s, the one-design dinghy whose class association I would one day oversee as executive director. I wasn't the best sailor on Cape Cod, but I was holding my own with the best, and some of those guys were the top competitors in the country. And I was on the cusp of the all-important high school years; if I wanted to get serious about sailing, I had to decide soon. The Cape Cod Academy, the small private school in Osterville, Massachusetts, that I attended because my mother was a teacher there, didn't have a sailing team. I'd started playing lacrosse and made varsity as an eighth-grader (I was big for my age, and the team needed bodies), and I'd reached a point where I thought sailing might be taking a backseat in my life.

The summer before my freshman year, I went on a student trip to Alaska. We spent several weeks backpacking in the Brooks Range and Denali National Park. I made passing mentions in my journal of the caribou and bears we spotted and the icy lakes we jumped into, but mostly I filled the pages with impassioned entries about how much I missed sailing. I began to understand what it meant to me. I couldn't wait to get back on the water.

After my freshman year at Cape Cod Academy, where my class

had all of eight kids in it, my parents and I talked about my going away to school. They wanted me to broaden my horizons. At home, I was mostly alone with my little sister. Ninety percent of the houses on the lake were unoccupied during the off-season. When I was younger, I had enjoyed roaming the shoreline, hopping over beached docks, bushwhacking through the woods, finding owl pellets to dissect under a microscope. But by age fifteen, the appeal of digging through bird regurgitations waned, and the lake started feeling desolate and dull. I got excited about going away to school—and especially about being on a high school sailing team.

As soon as I saw St. George's School, in Middletown, Rhode Island, just north of Newport, the epicenter of American sailing, I knew it was where I wanted to be. It had a Gothic-style chapel, brick dormitories with gabled roofs, and broad playing fields on a hill over-looking a crescent-shaped beach with surfable waves. On move-in day, I quickly shooed my parents out of my dorm room.

Several hours later, I called them from the hall phone to tell them I wanted to come home. But by the second day, as was my habit with new things, I was in love. I'd connected with some boys I had sailed against during the summer, and we had instantly bonded. Before long, I had friends from Saudi Arabia and Paris. The student body included the grandson of Jacques Cousteau; the grandson of Rhode Island senator Claiborne Pell; and the nephew, rumor had it, of the head of the Japanese mob—but there were plenty of regular kids, too, and many were there on scholarships.

The St. George's team was one of the oldest high school sailing programs in the country. Our clubhouse was the Ida Lewis Yacht Club, set in a nineteenth-century lightkeeper's house on a rocky is-land in Newport Harbor and connected to the mainland by a long walkway. I couldn't believe my good fortune. My parents had taken me to see the 1983 America's Cup race in Newport, and now I was sailing those same waters. And my team was excellent; during my years there, we won the New England conference several times, and we made it to the national finals.

Though I wasn't at the top of the national high school rankings, I was good enough to get a call from Scott Iklé, the head sailing coach at Hobart and William Smith Colleges in upstate New York, at a time when recruiting was almost unheard of in my sport. He said he wanted me to come sail for him. I was ecstatic. That Hobart was a small liberal arts school with a beautiful leafy campus on the shore of thirty-eight-mile-long Seneca Lake made it an easy decision.

When I arrived as a freshman, I thought I was the man. I had been *recruited*. I had it all figured it out. And that first fall, I was very fast. I could compete with anybody on the team. I was good at boat handling, which was a big part of sailing well. But I wasn't willing to work on the things that would have made me a stronger competitor—maybe even a contender for a spot in the Olympics. I should have been developing more of an awareness of what was happening on the racecourse and working on controlling my emotions in the heat of a race. And I would have benefited greatly from admitting that there were parts of sailing that I didn't understand. I did none of those things. More than anything, I wanted to be seen as accomplished, on my game, but that was a façade. By my sophomore year, the usual college distractions—parties and girls and the fraternity I had joined—had taken much of my attention away from sailing and classes. I was flailing both academically and on the water. It was my fault, but I blamed Coach Iklé.

Things were turning around for me in the fall of my junior year, but an accident at the start of the spring season halted whatever progress I had made. Every winter, we stored the Hobart sailboats on racks at the top of a bluff above the docks and the shingled, barn-shaped boathouse. In early spring, the team got together to haul them down to the water. When I climbed up on one boat in the middle of the stack, the weight of the snow that was still on them made the whole rack collapse. A nearly two-hundred-pound dinghy landed on my back. That entire spring, my back muscles were in spasm; it was hard to move or sleep. I didn't do enough to work at recovery, and I lost the whole season, including important events that might have propelled me toward doing a possible Olympic campaign. I was still on the team my senior year, but I was often on the bench—fuming at Coach Iklé for not giving me the starts I believed I deserved.

Meanwhile, I'd started coaching during the summers, first at the Mantoloking Yacht Club on the New Jersey shore and then back home at the Hyannis Yacht Club. After my junior and senior years, I coached the children's programs at the Chicago Yacht Club, just off Lake Shore Drive in the city's heart. I loved it. For the first time in a long while, I was fired up to learn. I read everything I could about being a teacher and a coach. At long last, I dedicated myself to understanding the technical aspects of sailing—the *why*—that I had ignored for so long. I didn't want the kids under my watch to make the mistakes I had made.

My passion for sailing shifted to coaching, and I started to think I might want to make a career of it. I had no postgraduation plans, much to parents' dismay, so I proposed that the Chicago Yacht Club keep me on year-round. I could coach high school sailing teams and teach classes that would generate enough revenue to cover my salary. They said, "Fine. Prove it." So, I went to work.

That first winter, I was sent to represent the Chicago Yacht Club at a national sailing symposium being held on Shelter Island in San Diego. I was wide-eyed. It was my first "business trip," and I'd left frigid Lake Michigan to go to a beachside hotel. The gathering of sailing professionals, vendors, and coaches featured on-water equipment demos and speakers. One of those speaking was Scott Iklé, my former coach at Hobart. I was excited to see him—it would be the first time since graduation—and I thought he'd be excited to see me, too.

After the morning presentations, we all walked across the hotel parking lot to the beach, where vendors had set up boats and training accessories for us to try out. I fell in with a group that included Scott.

"What are you doing now?" he asked.

I told him I was coaching fulltime for the Chicago Yacht Club.

"Really," he said.

"Yeah, I love it. And I think I'm actually going to try to make it a career—you know, coaching."

He slowed his pace. I slowed, too.

"That's a big mistake," he said. "You're not going to be very good at this. This isn't for you."

He walked on. I froze in place. I don't think he meant to be cruel—he was just being a straight shooter, as usual—but his opinion stung. I had no idea what he thought he saw in me that made me unsuitable for coaching. But I already knew that nearly everything I did from then on would be to show him he was wrong.

My sister Jennifer was by then a top sailor at St. Mary's College of Maryland, a small state school on the shores of a tributary of the Potomac. I'd competed against St. Mary's when I sailed for Hobart, and over the years, I'd gotten friendly with the team's head coach, Adam Werblow. That spring in 2003, Adam called me to suggest I apply for an assistant coaching post there. I wasn't sure I was ready for college coaching, but I interviewed while I was on campus for Jennifer's graduation. Adam offered me the job. It meant a pay cut, but I decided to take it. St. Mary's happened to be Hobart's biggest rival. It was not lost on me that I'd now be going up against Scott Iklé.

Adam and Scott had very different approaches to coaching. Scott was well-read but tended to be by-the-book, academic, and dry. His idea of discipline was to give you the silent treatment if you made him unhappy. There was little room for input from the team. Adam was also very knowledgeable, but he coached more by experience. He was relaxed and funny, and he was always asking questions, not just to stimulate dialog, but because he genuinely wanted to know what team members thought. He looked for ways to empower them. Returning members even ran tryouts and chose their new teammates.

I certainly admired parts of Scott's philosophy. He was very interested in sports psychology, for instance, and introduced me to creative thinkers like then–Chicago Bulls coach Phil Jackson, who incorporated spiritualism into his X's and O's. But I was also attracted to Adam's fun, low-key manner. My goal was to blend the best of both of them and maybe throw in a handful of Bill Belichick and a dollop of Terry Francona, my two Boston coaching idols.

I worked mostly with the St. Mary's women's team and often ran into Molly O'Bryan, an assistant coach at the US Naval Academy, at regattas. She had deep blue-green eyes, brown hair, freckles, and a great smile—and she was a fantastic sailor. She'd been an All-American skipper for the University of Hawaii and had led them to the 2001 ICSA Women's National Championship. She needed a dog sitter while she was at one of our home regattas, and Adam suggested me. When she came to pick up her dog, we talked for hours in my basement apartment. She was warm and intelligent and easygoing. By the time she left, I was smitten.

In 2006, Molly decided to try for the 2008 Olympics, competing in the doublehanded 470 class. That meant leaving her job and training out of Annapolis Harbor. Navy asked me whether I'd be interested in taking over Molly's coaching position. I felt like I still had much to learn at St. Mary's, and I hated to leave Adam, but I hated the idea of not being with Molly more. Plus, Annapolis had a lot more going for it than sleepy St. Mary's.

Navy's heritage was both thrilling and daunting. The Naval School was established in 1845 on a ten-acre army post at the confluence of the Severn River and the Chesapeake Bay, the same site occupied by the academy's sprawling campus. Dinghy racing became an intercollegiate sport at Navy in the spring of 1939, and since then, the sailing team had won the Leonard M. Fowle Trophy ten times—more than any other school in the country. For the past decade or so, though, the team had struggled.

I ASSISTED HEAD COACH GAVIN O'HARE, a Naval Academy alum who'd arrived in 2003 to try to right the listing team. Although he had for the most part done an incredible job of recruiting, the results were not there. Navy did have a talented women's team, but the program hadn't qualified in twelve years for a coed championship, the oldest national championship and the one considered to be the most prestigious.

I spent that first fall getting to know Gavin and the players, and trying to get a handle on the sailing department's complicated hierarchy. It was a strange soup of personnel: military commanders and lieutenants, civilian coaches for both the offshore and intercollegiate dinghy team, plus staff who presided over the academy's sail-training program. (Until 2007, all midshipmen had to learn how to sail.) On top of that, the program had a very active and vocal alumni group.

The entire department met weekly in the Robert Crown Sailing Center, a modern riverfront building with big windows overlooking Navy's impressive fleet of some 250 sailboats. Beyond them were the gray "Yard Patrol" mini-destroyers that served as training vessels. As one meeting got under way in December, I realized the commander and Gavin were no-shows. Halfway through the session, the commander poked his head into the room and said, "John, can I see you for a moment?"

I went out to the hall. He told me Gavin was going to be leaving his position.

"So, moving forward, you're in charge. You'll be our head coach on an interim basis."

He reached out to shake my hand. "We expect big things from you, and hopefully you'll work your way off that interim tag."

I was floored. Now, at twenty-eight, I was the youngest varsity head coach at Navy. Not only that, but the academy was hosting the national championships that spring, a huge undertaking for any school, and even more challenging at a military institution, with all of its bewildering red tape. I'd be overseeing that, too.

Before I could focus on getting geared up for the nationals regatta, though, I had to come up with a plan to get the team out of the doldrums. I decided that we would focus on one skill set and get really good at it, and then we'd build on that. I told them I didn't care about results; they would come. Not surprisingly, the players had tremendous discipline—these were student-athletes who had survived the grueling Plebe Summer boot camp—and they threw themselves into the new training program. We found success right away. For the first time in a dozen years, we qualified for all the spring championships, then went on to finish eighth in team racing and ninth in coeds at our home venue nationals.

By the time the fall 2007 season started, Navy had taken the "interim" off my title and offered me more money. And then in June 2008, I got a call from Stanford University. They were looking for a head coach. At first, I thought there was no way. I was just getting going with Navy; things were moving in the right direction. Molly and I had gotten married and were happy living in Annapolis. But since I had plans to go to San Francisco to put on a Club 420 clinic and coach at the US Youth Sailing Championships in late June, I thought I might as well talk to Stanford while I was there. If nothing else, it would be good practice. I did the interview with Ray Purpur, the deputy director of athletics, but left feeling it hadn't gone well. I knew I hadn't made an effort to put my best foot forward; I didn't even wear a coat and tie.

The San Francisco Yacht Club, across from the city on the tip of the Tiburon Peninsula, was hosting the youth championships on a course set off the Berkeley coast. The views of Angel Island and the San Francisco skyline and both bay bridges were spectacular—and the sailing conditions were superb. After a couple of days there, I started to think maybe I wanted that Stanford job after all. I was angry at myself for not taking the interview more seriously.

Midway through the youth regatta, I got a call from Purpur. Stanford wanted to offer me the job. The money was good, and the head coach position came with housing—a huge perk, especially in Palo Alto, where the cost of living was one of the highest in the country.

Molly and I talked it over. We liked the idea of having a traditional collegiate experience—even though Molly would be traveling a lot as part of the US Sailing Team. She had just missed qualifying for the 2008 Olympics but was already aiming for the 2012 games in London. I was intrigued by the idea of being in that mecca of innovation; I wondered whether I might be able to tap into some of that Silicon Valley technology and bring it to a sailing program.

And it was *Stanford*. I couldn't deny the pull that name had on me. I'd be part of the nation's best overall athletic program, and I'd have a chance to leave a lasting mark. No West Coast college sailing team in recent history had been competitive on the national stage. I could be the coach who changed that.

I accepted the job.

The team I took over had plenty of talent but little discipline. I made it clear from the start that the parties were going to end. We were athletes; we were going to work hard. The captains revolted, and several players quit shortly after I arrived. Now I had to recruit their replacements.

10

I rode my bike across campus, enjoying the cool of morning and the way rain the night before had heightened the scent of the cedar and eucalyptus trees that lined the still-wet streets and walkways. I was headed to my office to catch up with Clinton and Belle after a busy weekend. They'd been in Cleveland on Lake Erie to coach and compete in US Sailing's Team National Championships, a semi-pro event that was open to postgrads, and I'd scrambled between three different regattas on the East Coast. My first stop had been the Club 420 Mid-Atlantic Championships in Niantic, Connecticut. After a day and a half there, I'd driven back to Boston to pick up the players competing in a regatta at the Coast Guard Academy in New London, Connecticut. Then I'd returned to Boston and hopped on a flight to Baltimore to catch up with the women competing at St. Mary's.

I parked my bike and went upstairs. Belle and Clinton were just starting to tell me about their regatta when my cell rang. I saw it was Rick Singer.

"Sorry," I said to them as I picked up the phone.

"Hey, Rick."

"Hey, John, I wanted—"

I couldn't hear him—the damn cell service. I stood up to start the trek outside and gestured to Clinton and Belle that I'd be right back. I held the phone to my ear as I walked, straining to make out what Singer was saying. I heard the words "bad news" as I stepped outside.

"The bad news is that Mia decided that she doesn't really want to go to Stanford. She really wants to go to Vanderbilt. So they're not going to move forward."

"Okay."

"And they're not going to make their five hundred thousand payment to you. But I'm, you know, I'm still going to be supportive. So, I can, I will figure out what can make sense so I can pay you, you know, one hundred—maybe two hundred thousand. Would that be okay . . . pay that to you?"

"Yes, that would be—that would be fantastic," I said. I was so relieved. I'd used Singer's money to hire Belle and our boatwright, but that had been only enough to cover them for one year. If I didn't find more funding, I'd have to let them go.

"Okay, and then because, you know, I know we gave five hundred thousand for Molly. But I, I don't think I can do the five hundred thousand paying to you just out of my own pocket, my own foundation," he said, speaking quickly. "So—if you're okay, I'll, I'll get back to you, one hundred—or two hundred thousand, I'll pay to you. And then that way, hopefully, it, you know, keeps our relationship alive. And I apologize for this whole thing."

"Yeah, no, not a problem," I said, not sure what he was apologizing for.

"Okay with you?"

"Yeah, yeah, absolutely."

Singer then asked if he should write out the check to me or to Stanford. I told him it should go to Stanford, just as the others had.

I hung up. I was puzzled by his question about the check and by how flustered he had sounded, but mostly I was excited to hear he planned to donate again. I wouldn't lose my assistants.

In a few months, I would find out why Singer had seemed so jumpy on that call. He was by then a cooperating witness in the case the government had dubbed "Operation Varsity Blues." The FBI had been listening in and recording our call. The prosecution would eventually use a partial transcript of this and our next two phone conversations as evidence against me.

Three days later, on October 5, I was back in my office when Singer called again. I answered and immediately left my office to make my way to better reception.

"Sorry . . . swamped . . . in Boston right now. Here's a question for—or this is what I'd like—if we . . . make happen. I will—"

His voice was garbled.

"Okay," I said.

"—send you one hundred sixty thousand. And can we make . . . the next student that we have?"

"Because what, what do I normally give . . . how much?"

"Uh," I said as I walked.

"The last . . . I gave you—five hundred, right?"

I reached the stairwell.

"Okay. So, could . . . the one-sixty count toward the five hundred—next year or something?"

I pushed the exit door and walked out to the alley, squinting in the bright sun. I could hear him.

"Yes. Yeah, yeah, that could work." I had no idea what I was agreeing to.

"So, okay, so—so essentially what you're saying is . . . I just want to make sure because I've done this before. And I just need to make sure."

"Yeah."

"So, so I'll send you $160,000. And then for next year . . . get a kid, and normally we pay you five hundred. That one-sixty will count as like, I don't know, you call it a deposit for the next year's kid."

"Right," I said, thinking *deposit* was strange word to use. "So you would go for four-twenty?"

"Four-twenty," he said. Then he laughed. "It would be three-forty, right?"

"Three-forty," I said. "Sorry."

"Right, so we agree, okay, so you, okay with, then we would pay you—three hundred forty thousand the following year."

"Yes. Yeah."

"Okay, great. Then I'll get that taken care of. Thanks for being patient with me. And it's great—it's great working with you."

"Yeah," I said. "No problem."

Months later, I would understand that the FBI needed me to say those dollar figures out loud. They needed Singer to ask me to do the math. I'd also learn that they had pressed him to suggest he send the money directly to me. They'd likely hoped Singer would get me to say, "Sure, just write that fat check to me"—and, probably to their great disappointment, I hadn't taken the bait.

But I also hadn't asked questions. Here is what I should have said: "What are you talking about, Rick? What do you mean *a deposit* for next year's kid? Why is it a *deposit*?" As with so many of my conversations with Singer and other donors, I just wanted to wrap things up and get off the phone. I didn't listen. And that fact destroyed me.

I EMAILED ADAM SCHNEBERGER, THE ATHLETICS director in development who oversaw sailing at the time—Heather Owen had by then been promoted—to tell him the good news about Singer's gift.

"Great news on Rick," he replied. "I think it would be wise to have him sign a pledge document for the gifts."

Donors choosing to spread out large donations over several years often did that. I told him I would ask. Singer emailed back that he wasn't interested in signing any pledges.

Singer called again on October 24, catching me in my office once more with Belle and Clinton. We were editing video, making slides, and preparing talks for that afternoon's weekly team meeting. We only had a few hours to get everything done. I told them I'd be right back and started walking toward the exit.

"So, what I want to—what I want to touch base with is tomorrow, I'm gonna mail out a check for $160,000."

"Awesome," I said.

". . . what you asked for . . ." He was breaking up. "But what I wanted to—sure that we're confirmed . . . going forward . . . have a spot with you . . . probably . . . athlete like Molly—"

"Okay," I said, trotting down the stairs. I thought I lost him until I stepped outside and could hear him again.

"And then here's the other thing I—I have a quick question," he said. "Maybe you can help me. Now I have another kid, who potentially is from—and is potentially—this is—wants to be a sailor—lookin' to go East, to sail—from Seattle."

"Okay."

"But I need to create a new profile. And I just have no idea of like—What are the best regattas that she can participate in? Can you help me with that?"

"Yeah, sure." I looked at my watch. I didn't have time for this. "She's a Northwest sailor? So she's Seattle?"

"Yes."

"Okay. And—"

"If you—if you could email me some of those, that would be fabulous."

"No problem," I said. That was easy. I often advised younger sailors about which regattas were best to attend.

"And then, just going forward, again, I will bring you another student athlete just like Molly, who's n-not a—a sailor but—make things work, 'cause she'll be really a student—if that's okay."

"Yeah. No, that's fine." I was only half-listening. God, Singer could talk. All I wanted to do was wrap this up and get back upstairs.

Singer's $160,000 check arrived a few days later. I didn't open the by now familiar envelope. I took it downstairs and handed it off to Adam.

"Fantastic," he said. "Thank you."

I emailed Singer a list of regattas that his client could consider entering. I thought I was being helpful. The FBI, who by now was watching my every move and intercepting every communication, would use this exchange to allege that I was conspiring with Rick Singer to create a falsified athletic profile.

Meanwhile, I had bigger things on my mind than lending a hand to Singer's client. I had to prepare for a major athletics department strategic review meeting during which I, like every head coach, would get thirty minutes alone with the senior staff, including Bernard Muir, to talk about my team's successes, goals, and budgets. That was a big deal. I rarely got to speak to the higher-ups.

But a few days before the meeting, Molly and I had to rush Nora to the hospital, where she was admitted to the Pediatric Intensive Care Unit with severe bronchitis. We'd been through this before—every cold Nora caught seemed to go straight to her lungs—but it made it no less frightening. Molly and I took turns staying with her. We were so relieved that after eight days, Nora was getting back to her old self, smiling and giggling and using her big eyes to ham it up with the nurses, even though she was still hooked up to oxygen tubes and monitors. On the afternoon of the big meeting, Molly and I swapped places in Nora's room so I could head over to the athletics building. Still wearing my hospital visitor badge, I hurried up to Bernard's office.

Bernard, Heather Owen, Beth Goode, and Patrick Dunkley, plus Tommy Gray, who handled media relations, and Brian Talbott, the chief financial officer for athletics, were seated at the round table. Bernard had positioned his leather captain's chair opposite a massive, wall-mounted TV. An NCAA basketball game was on, with the sound muted.

"It's a good thing you wore your name badge, or we wouldn't have known who you were," Bernard said to me as I joined them at the table.

That got a few chuckles. No one asked why I had been a visitor at Children's Hospital. I distributed a handout to the group about the sailing program, bulleting information about the Leonard M. Fowle Trophy and our sport's six national championships. Bernard's eyes never left the basketball game while I spoke.

"So, we just won a national championship," I said. "Which was great."

The group looked at me blankly.

"One of our sophomores won the women's singlehanded national championship on Lake Michigan. It was a really big win for her."

"Does that count?" Beth asked. "You know, since it's not during your championship season?"

"Yes. It counts," I said. I was exasperated. I'd been at Stanford for eleven years. Sailing wasn't a new varsity sport, and I'd just gone over our two-season structure. "It's a real national championship. We have six. Three in the fall, three in the spring."

More blank looks.

"She didn't get any acknowledgment," I went on, "and, um, I was thinking it would be nice if maybe something could be posted on social media to, you know, recognize her accomplishment."

"I don't know," Bernard said, still glued to the game. "Maybe. Maybe we could do something. Tommy, maybe do something on Twitter?"

I went on to talk about the significant strides we had made in improving team culture, how I was bringing in sports psychologists and fitness and nutrition experts. I said I'd instituted a daily check-in survey with the players so I could better understand how they were feeling mentally and physically each day. Knowing whether they were stressed about exams or exhausted after an all-nighter helped me plan my approach with each player at practice. I said I thought it was making a difference. Bernard continued to stare at the television.

Then I started to talk about our budget. "I'm hoping to hire another assistant coach. I'd need to fund-raise for that."

For the first time, Bernard glanced my way.

"You've done a great job fund-raising, John," he said. "Keep it up."

11

FEBRUARY 2019

I was sitting with the women's team at a pizza place in Dulles Airport's Terminal C, furtively checking my phone every few seconds. It had been two weeks since the FBI and IRS had showed up at my house. Molly's friend Anne Wright had gotten back to us about a lawyer she knew. He'd told her he could talk to me during the team's DC layover and that he'd email me when it was a good time to call. When his message finally appeared, I left my bags with the players and said I'd be back. I turned right and headed down Terminal D.

"So, tell me what's going on," he said when I reached him. I gave him a condensed version of my story as I walked the dingy gray carpet, weaving through crowds.

"Wow," he said. "That's, that's incredible. But, I'm a corporate attorney. I'm really not the right guy to help you with this case. I'm afraid I don't know anything about federal bribery."

"Neither do I."

"What I do know, though, is you don't want to use a court-appointed attorney for this thing. You need someone who really understands that area of law. It's extremely complicated, and it doesn't come up very often. You need to find somebody who specializes in it, who will really advocate for you."

"So you think I should get a different lawyer—"

"It's going to cost you, but I think it will definitely be worth it."

"Yeah. I understand."

"This is going to be very, very tough. I'm sorry I can't help."

I thanked him and hung up, thoroughly shaken by what he had said. I'd been scared before, but now I was petrified. If John Amabile, my court-appointed lawyer, wasn't right for me, then who was? How would I find that person? And how the hell would I pay for him or her? I got to the end of the D gates, turned around, and walked back through the terminal. The pressing, low ceiling, the stream of people, the constant unintelligible announcements all fueled my rising panic. I felt like I couldn't take in a full breath.

I realized then that I had no choice but to get my parents involved. I'd hoped to resolve this mess without their ever knowing about it, but it was clear that I couldn't handle this alone. I needed their advice and support. I returned to the restaurant where the team was still hanging out, gathered my bags, and told them I'd meet them at the gate. At the far end of the airport tram station, I found a quiet corner and called home. My father answered. I fought to keep it together as I told him what had happened.

"Oh my god, John," he said.

"I know." I saw the team coming down the escalator. I waved to them and then turned my back. "I'm terrified."

"Okay. We'll handle this. We will. Absolutely. But I think you're right. You can't use a court-appointed lawyer. Not for this. Let me see if I can find you someone."

"I can't pay for it."

"We won't worry about that now. We'll work it out."

We planned to talk again once I got to Charleston.

"Can I tell your mother?" he said.

It pained me to picture my mother's reaction. Reluctantly, I said yes.

I jumped on the tram and raced to the gate, just making it before the plane's door closed. When we landed, I picked up the rental car and drove the team to the hotel, which was just down the street from the sailing venue. When everyone was settled, I called home again. This time my mother answered.

"Jesus fucking Christ, John! How the hell could they do this to you?!"

That was pretty much exactly what I thought she would say. For an elementary school teacher, she had the mouth of a South Boston ironworker.

My father got on the phone. He told me he'd called the Boston law firm Nixon Peabody, which both he and my brother-in-law had recently used. They were working on finding someone for me.

There was no point in trying to sleep. I sat up in bed in the blue glow of my laptop and searched for information about bribery cases. There were dozens of hits about the NCAA basketball recruiting scandal that had been so much in the news. Coaches were charged with accepting bribes to influence star athletes' choice of schools, shoe sponsors, and agents. They were facing prison time and huge fines. I couldn't understand why bribery was being used in these cases; they were no more government employees than I was.

Then I saw this in a *New York Times* story: "Basketball coaches are not usually thought of as government officials, but a 1984 statute—aimed at helping prosecutors police local governments and private organizations that receive federal funding—means those working even at private universities can effectively become public employees."

Stanford received hundreds of millions of dollars in government grants and loans. I flashed back to that morning in my kitchen when the IRS agent had told me I'd broken the law and reminded me the university received federal funds. It had gone over my head then, but now it was sickeningly clear why it mattered.

I watched the clock until it was time to get up, then went to a grocery store to pick up food for the team. After a quick stop for a cup of coffee, I swung back to the hotel to get the team. I had to be a coach now: positive, supportive, communicative. Everything else had to be shut off.

Under a hazy sky, the players and I walked down the long, steep ramp to the College of Charleston sailing center, set where the tidal Cooper River empties into Charleston Harbor. This venue was notorious for having a lot of surface current. I'd always liked coaching there, trying to figure out how to play the tricky conditions. Sailing in current is like being on a conveyor belt—every boat is going the same speed. One way to vary speed when current is more dominant than wind is to head for different water depths. Shallower water has less current; deeper water, more. The course that morning was set just to the left of the USS *Yorktown*, a nearly nine-hundred-foot World War II–era aircraft carrier and museum. I knew there was a deep water channel to one side of the ship. I'd tell my players to get to the shallow side if they felt the current was hurting them, and to the deeper side if it was helping.

I went off to the coaches' meeting, where I learned that because of a storm forecasted for Sunday, the organizers were hoping to complete all the racing in one day. I let the team know about the possible abbreviated schedule. Then we found our boats and started going through the usual prerace inspections, searching for any weakness that could potentially lead to a midrace breakdown. The sailors checked the knots in the hiking straps to make sure they were secure and examined the rubber universals in the tiller extensions to make sure they weren't cracked. They wrapped electrical tape around all the ring dings, the circular fittings that attach the main sheet and jib sheet blocks, to show they had checked them and to keep them from falling out. A thorough inspection was essential. If a boat broke down in the middle of a race and it was something you could have spotted before you launched, the protest committee wouldn't award you breakdown points (the average of your other finishes that day). When everyone had finished, we got together and lifted each boat from their bows, draining their air tanks to make sure they were as light as possible. Then I talked with the team about strategy, given that the event was probably going to be condensed into one day.

"We need to make sure that after lunch, we're solidifying points," I said. "We want to be going for the win. That might mean taking some risks a little earlier than normal."

I also took some time to speak alone with Camille, a freshman driving in her first college event. I told her it wasn't about results today. I wanted her to focus on getting off the starting line and communicating well. I wished her luck and told her I believed in her.

Then I climbed aboard the coach boat with my colleagues from other teams and headed out on the water. Coach boats are unlike any other sports sideline. We aren't allowed to have any interaction with a sailor during a race; there is no yelling out strategy, encouragement, or criticism. Onboard, we watch, take notes, and shoot video. After each race, the players sail up to the side of the coach boat, and coaches either hand them notes or lean over the side to tell them what we observed. I usually tried to point out something a player had done well in the previous race and suggest something that would be important to do in the next one.

When I was first starting coaching, I eavesdropped on my colleagues as they talked to their sailors—not just to find out what they were saying, but how they were saying it. I'd learned over the years to tailor my comments to individual players: some needed confidence-boosting, some wanted to know what they had done wrong, some didn't want to hear a thing.

Around noon that day, the breeze shut off, and the current took over. Racing got marginal, at best. The organizers decided to head in for lunch and to wait for the breeze to fill in again. When it did, it was out of the east, so the course was moved to an area south of the marina called Crab Bank, a crescent of offshore sand where the water was shallower and current was much less a factor. We finished strong, taking no lower than third place in the last six races, and in the end, Stanford was second overall. I was happy for the team; they'd sailed very well in tricky conditions. And I'd been caught up in the action enough to forget about my situation.

But it all came crashing back when I got to my hotel room and called home. My father told me he'd talked to a lawyer, Robert Fisher, at Nixon Peabody, who could likely help. The firm was doing due diligence to make sure they had no conflicts of interest with Stanford.

The following Monday, back in Palo Alto, I filled out forms to become a Nixon Peabody client. The retainer was $25,000. My sister Jennifer and her husband, David, generously offered to help me make the payment. I had so little experience with lawyers that I thought that $25,000 might cover the whole thing. Instead, I burned through that by the end of the first week.

Later that day, I heard from Rob Fisher. He said he was tied up with another case in Washington, DC (representing, I found out later, someone who was the subject of Special Counsel Robert

Mueller's Russia investigation), so it would be a few more days before he could focus on my case.

"In the meantime, it's fine to have John Amabile handle the first meeting with the US Attorneys," Rob said.

"I know all of those guys," he added. "I worked in the US Attorney's Office in Boston for ten years. The guy in charge, Eric Rosen, was my mentee. Let me talk to them and find out what's going on."

I felt much better after talking to Rob. Now I had a high-powered lawyer who knew everybody on the other side. I felt sure that soon enough, everything would be straightened out.

I knew John Amabile planned to meet with the US Attorney's Office at midday on Tuesday. I was on edge all morning waiting to hear from him. He called just as I was approaching the Stanford boathouse entrance. Instead of driving in, I continued past it to a parking lot across from the public boat ramp. I pulled into a spot near rows of trailered boats.

"Okay, so I want to go through what the government is charging you with," he said. "Now, there is a chance that they are bluffing, and we could ignore this and see what they do next. We do have options."

My pulse quickened. I turned off the engine.

"Okay."

"Here are the charges. Honest services fraud. Tax fraud. Wire fraud."

Tax fraud? Wire fraud? I'd heard of these things in mobster movies.

"Each of these counts carries a prison sentence of twenty years, and then each would carry some significant fines, as well."

Jesus, what? Twenty years? Or did he say twenty years, *each*?

"They do have recordings of phone calls between you and Rick Singer," he went on. "I have not heard them. Now, I want you to know they are willing to give you a deal. And that deal would be twenty-four months in prison. So you would knock all of this down to twenty-four months if you plead guilty to an Information."

"An Information?" I asked weakly.

"It's basically the government's summary of what happened. So if you took this deal, you would be giving up your right to a grand jury, and you would be pleading guilty to the information the government now has."

"I would have to say I'm guilty?"

"Correct. You would plead guilty."

"And I would go to jail—

"They're offering you twenty-four months."

"I, uh—" I felt lightheaded.

"Now, they want you to know that if you decide not to take the deal, you can expect the government to raid your house in the near future at 6 a.m., at gunpoint."

I had a vision of Nicholas in his Little Blue Truck pajamas, standing at the top of the stairs wailing while people with guns went through the house. My stomach rolled.

"They would likely handcuff you and pull you out of the house and put you in their car. They would then take you to the nearest district court to arraign you. And then you would have to go to Boston to go to trial."

"Boston?"

"Correct. Now, they need an answer by 5 p.m. on Friday. Whether you're going to take the plea deal or not."

"Friday. You mean this Friday?"

"That's correct."

Amabile kept talking, going over each charge in detail, but I was only half-comprehending: honest services fraud because I somehow hadn't done my job for Stanford; mail fraud because I had used the US Postal Service; tax fraud because I didn't know why—something about Singer's nonprofit foundation. I didn't understand how any of these things applied to me. The sun beat through my car windshield. Sweat dripped into my eyes and off my chin.

"Now, as I said, the government could be bluffing and just trying to get you to jump on a plea deal. But we have to respond by Friday. You understand?"

"Yes."

"I'll give you a little time to process all of this. If you have questions, just ask. Let's talk tomorrow, and we can go over everything again. And of course, you shouldn't tell anyone about this. Otherwise, you could be charged with obstruction of justice."

I hung up, grabbed the steering wheel with both hands, and screamed. And then my screams turned into sobs. I cried hard for ten minutes. I wanted to disappear. I wanted to shrink down to a speck of nothing. Everything I ever thought about myself—that I was a good person, a trustworthy person, a person of honor, a person who would not cut the fucking tags off a mattress, for fuck's sake—was being questioned and attacked. Suddenly I was being called a criminal.

And now Molly and Nicholas and Nora, the three people I loved most in the world, were being dragged into this nightmare. How was I going to get them out of it? How were they going to sustain themselves if I went to jail for two years? I would fall on a sword for them. I didn't care what happened to me. I needed to get my wife and kids out of this. From where I was parked, I could see Molly's PYSF office. I knew she was sitting in there at her desk. How was I going to tell her? What if she wanted to leave me?

When I had composed myself, I made the short drive over to her office. I knew she would see I had been crying; there was nothing I could do about that. I walked in, telling myself to keep it together, to speak calmly. She was sitting at her desk.

"What?" she said with alarm when she saw me.

"That lawyer called. He told me what I'm charged with. It's unbelievable. It's like three counts of fraud or something, and—" I struggled to get the next words out. "They would each get me twenty years in jail."

Her face fell.

"But he said I can make a deal. If I plead . . . plead guilty and then I would . . . he said then I'd go to jail for two years."

"What? Two years? You'd go to jail? Are you serious?"

"Yes."

"You have to say you're guilty?"

"Yes."

"But you didn't do anything wrong!"

"I know that. But the lawyer said they're giving me a way out."

"This is insane!" she said.

"I know."

"And you have to decide by Friday? Can you get more time?"

"I don't know. I don't think so."

"Well, did you ask him that?"

"No."

"But you have this other Boston lawyer now. Can't he help?"

"I don't know," I said.

We looked at each other without speaking.

"I feel terrible—," I said. My voice broke. "For dragging you into this."

"That doesn't matter right now. That's not the important thing. You have that other lawyer. He's really good, right? Your dad said that. And he'll help."

"Yeah, maybe."

"When do you talk to him again?"

"I'm not sure. He said today, I think. Or tomorrow."

"Well, did you ask?"

"Yes—I don't know!" I covered my face with my hands.

"It's okay. We will work this out," Molly said with conviction. "We will. This is not the end of the world."

I looked at her. I loved her so much. But it did feel like the end of the world.

We both had to get ready to run our practices. I hugged her and made the five-minute drive back to the sailing center. Rob Fisher called me just as I pulled in to park. I tried to tell him everything John Amabile had said to me. I was sure I was getting a lot of it wrong.

"I'll try to get them to slow this thing down," he said. "I can say you just became a client twenty-four hours ago and that I need time to look through the evidence, to help you make the decision. I think they'll do that for me. I'll call you tomorrow around this same time."

I took a few deliberate breaths and looked at myself in the rearview mirror. Everything had to seem normal now. I would walk into the boathouse. I would pull on my foul-weather gear, and I would go upstairs to meet with Clinton and Belle, as always. We'd talk about the wind and the current and our practice plan. When the team arrived, I would ask them how their days were going, if they were getting their projects and papers done. I'd read their moods. I'd do what I could to bolster their spirits if they seemed down, joke around if they appeared to be feeling playful. Then we would sail.

The next day, as the team was rigging the boats, I told Clinton and Belle I wasn't feeling well and asked if they could run drills while I stayed onshore. I was expecting that call from Rob and couldn't risk missing it if I was on the water. My phone rang just after the team sailed away from the dock.

"Listen John, I tried," Rob said, "but the deadline is still the end of day Friday. We need to get you to Boston."

I was stunned. I'd been sure he'd tell me he'd fixed it all somehow.

"Okay. I guess I can get a redeye after practice on Thursday," I said.

"Perfect."

After we hung up, I let John Amabile know I had decided to get my own lawyer. He wished me well.

On Thursday, Rob called me with more news.

"This case is bigger than we thought," he said. "I just heard that multiple coaches are involved."

"Other Stanford coaches?" I flashed back to seeing Singer at my door and thinking he might have been buzzed through to visit my colleagues.

"That I don't know. But it's clear to me that you're the only one of the group who is getting a deal without being a cooperating witness," he said.

I wasn't sure what that meant. Was that good?

"Also, I heard one of the tapes the government has. It's a call between you and Singer. He's talking about a donation. This guy is like a super informant. He's either reading from a script, or he's just really, really good at this. You can hear him trying to lock you into all of this stuff."

I thought back to those odd October calls.

"But it's also pretty obvious that you weren't paying attention to a lot of what he was saying. You were just yeah'ing him to death."

"That's exactly what it was," I said. "I couldn't hear him, so I was just like, 'Yeah, yeah, okay, yeah.'"

I wondered whether lousy cell service could be considered a defense.

"So, now I need you to grab everything that is possibly related to the case, even if you don't know if it's related. Handbooks from Stanford, your computer, your phone, of course. Everything needs to come."

"Okay," I said. "But, you know, I feel like if I could just explain things to Stanford—"

"That's not an option. Stanford has likely testified against you in front of the grand jury. And they will do it again if we go to trial."

I was crushed. Stanford had testified against me? They knew about Singer and the charges against me—and they were not on my side? All of these years I had bled Cardinal red, and they were not even willing to hear what I had to say? I paced up and down the dock while the team went through their drills out in the bay. Would I be taken into custody the moment I pleaded guilty? When would I see my family again? Would I go right to jail? Could my wife and kids visit me? Would I want them to?

Molly and I tried hard to make things feel normal for the kids on Thursday evening. We had dinner, and I packed for the redeye to Boston. We acted like Daddy was going off on another work trip.

"See you soon," Molly said at the door. I knew she was trying to keep it light, but I saw the pain in her eyes. "Have a good trip."

The kids waved and blew kisses. It was excruciating.

12

'd hoped to get some sleep on the flight to Boston, but mostly I just
stared out the window into the darkness, berating myself. When
the first streaks of gray and pink appeared low on the eastern horizon, I felt nauseated. I pulled my Red Sox hat low and slumped in
the seat as the plane started its bumpy descent for Logan Airport.

I walked out the door near baggage claim and was instantly jolted
awake by the frigid air. I'd brought only a light jacket. My father
pulled up to the curb, got out of the car, and hugged me.

"It's freezing," I said.

"California boy now," he said with a smile as he took my roller
bag from me. "Did you sleep?"

"Not at all," I said. "I could use some coffee."

We parked in downtown Boston, made a quick stop at a coffee shop, and walked down State Street to Exchange Place, the
forty-story glass tower where Nixon Peabody had its offices. On the
thirty-first floor, we stepped off the elevator into a sleek, airy lobby
outfitted with low-slung, modern furniture. My first thought was
expensive. Shortly after we told a receptionist who we were there
to see, Rob Fisher—dark suit, tortoiseshell glasses, groomed salt-
and-pepper short beard—appeared at the top of an open stairway.

I guessed he was in his mid-forties, just a few years older than me. We shook hands and went into a small conference room that had floor-to-ceiling windows and sweeping views of Boston Harbor. There were fresh croissants in a basket on a round table. Rob asked us to take seats. Another lawyer, Scott Seitz, athletic-looking and maybe a decade younger than Rob, came in and joined us.

"So let me walk you through what will happen today," Rob said. "We'll listen to your whole story, and then Scott and I will go over to the US Attorney's Office and talk to them and see what we can do. We need you to tell us everything. Don't hold back. And if you don't feel comfortable with your father in the room, it's okay to ask him to leave."

I said I had nothing to hide. My dad could stay.

"Our goal is that you would go sit with them for a proffer later."

"I don't know what that is."

A proffer, he said, would be my telling the prosecutors everything I know in exchange for immunity. I felt a rush of hope. Maybe this would all be over by the end of the day.

"This whole thing might very well be just a lack of knowledge on the government's part as to how admissions and recruiting works at Stanford," Rob said. "So, you would explain all of that to them."

First, though, he needed me to explain it to him and Scott. I spent the next hour or so telling them about recruiting—the pink envelopes, the Ranking and Justification forms, the timing. Scott took notes. They both asked questions about how and where I found prospects. I told them about the college nights I hosted and the youth regattas I scouted. I said that although college placement counselors were common in other better-funded sports, I had never used the services of one until Rick Singer walked into my office in October 2016.

"Tell us about him," Rob said.

"He was just like this really friendly guy. Easy to talk to. Super relaxed. He wanted to know all about the sailing program and recruiting. He seemed interested in everything I was doing."

I told them about Adam Cohen's endorsement and about the mystifying $500,000 donation that Singer said came from the Zhao family. Then I walked them through the Bodhi Patel saga, and the $110,000 Singer gave to the sailing program out of his pocket.

"He wanted to help me hire some assistants," I said. "He said explicitly that there were no strings attached to the donation. He wanted to support the sailing program. That was it."

Rob picked up a Stanford recruiting handbook I had brought along and began leafing through it. He stopped on a page near the front of the book.

"It says here the only stipulation about who you bring to admissions for a pink envelope is that the student can help your program. If all of this money goes to the school, it seems that you were just doing your job. You were helping your program. Right?"

"Yes," I said. "Definitely. That was my understanding."

"Maybe if the government saw this handbook."

"They'd see I was doing my job," I said. "But I really think all I need to do is talk to Stanford—"

"You'd be wasting your time. Stanford is circling the wagons right now."

Rob left to call the US Attorney's Office. Sandwiches were brought in. I forced one down, knowing my body needed the fuel. Scott asked me for my laptop so he could download my emails. When he had trouble doing it himself, he left with it to ask the firm's tech people to work on it. In a little while, one of them came back with my computer and a thumb drive.

Rob returned. "I think we'll be able to go there in a little bit. We're working on timing."

He and Scott went through my emails together, asking about exchanges I'd had with Singer, Heather Owen, Adam Cohen, and others. I explained each one.

I told them about Mia, the gymnast, and how Singer had presented her to me as someone eager to switch to sailing. And that he had called me in October to say she didn't want to go to Stanford, after all. That was the call when he said he wanted to donate $160,000 to the team—and promised there would be more coming after that.

"The call I heard," Rob said, nodding.

"But I couldn't hear him," I said. "We have terrible service in the athletic building. You have to go outside to take calls. You can ask anybody who works there. It's awful. So, I was walking while he was talking, just holding the phone to my ear and saying 'uh-huh,' or whatever, until I got outside."

"You clearly weren't paying attention."

"Can I see your phone, please?" Scott asked. He started scrolling through my text messages, stopping every few minutes to ask about conversations I'd had with Singer.

"Oh-oh," he said with a frown. "What's this one? You say, 'What kind of donation are we talking about? Could it be more than $500,000?'"

"I was just trying to get an idea of who we were dealing with. Singer said the family was wealthy. I was wondering what kind of potential they had to donate in the future. It was something I thought admissions might want to know."

Scott nodded slowly and then went back to my texts.

"What about this? You're asking Singer for Mia's athletics résumé. 'I need to know what sports she plays.' I mean, the government is going to have a field day with this. You're asking what sports this girl plays? After you've said she's an athletic recruit?"

"Besides *sailing*!" My father said with exasperation. It was the first time he'd spoken since I started telling my story.

"Right," I said, nodding at my dad. "Besides sailing. That's what I'm asking. What *other* sports she played. We'd already had conversations about her sailing experience, but I needed her full résumé before I could fill out the Athlete Ranking Form."

"See, this is where you start to get in trouble," Rob said. "They're going to cherry-pick these texts. And they're going to put them on a screen in front of the jury and not give any context. Then they have that taped phone call. They can just read the transcript of the call out loud and not play the actual recording. Reading it is very different from listening to it. It's clear in the recording that you can't hear him well and that you aren't paying attention through a lot of it—like you said—but it won't be clear to the jurors, who just have the transcript read to them.

"And because of the recorded calls, we'd be disinclined to put you on the stand."

"Oh? I wouldn't testify?"

"You can testify—it's your right to, but it's almost always a losing strategy, particularly in a case with calls."

"Okay," I said. I was both relieved and perplexed to hear I wouldn't be testifying in my own defense.

"The cross-examination would be just brutal. You saying it was 'bad phone reception'? How do you think a jury would receive that? They'd be like, 'Yeah, sure.' And since these text and phone conversations are just between you and Singer, Singer would get up there and say, 'He meant this.' And I wouldn't be able to put you on the stand to say, 'No, I didn't mean that.' And that makes it tough."

My father and I exchanged looks. This wasn't sounding good at all.

"Okay," Rob said. "Keep going. What happened next?"

"So, in February, the FBI and IRS came to my door," I said.

"And you let them in."

"Yes."

"Okay. Just for future reference, do not let them in. Ever. You have the right to say no. People don't know they can do that. Criminals know, but innocent people don't. You can just say you'd like to reschedule when you have your lawyer by your side. Because once they are in and asking questions, then they are going to have to write up a 302."

"A 302?"

"It's a summary of everything you said in the encounter based on their notes and their memory. There's no recording. So the 302, it's their interpretation of what was said, and it doesn't have to be verbatim. Of course, they're supposed to tell the truth, but they can write pretty much what they want. And you'll never see it."

I learned later that it was a long-standing FBI practice not to record interviews. In a 2006 review of the policy, the agency had determined that the presence of recording devices might "interfere with and undermine the successful rapport-building interviewing technique which the FBI practices." They had also found that "perfectly lawful and acceptable interviewing techniques do not always come across in recorded fashion to laypersons as proper means of obtaining information from defendants." No kidding. Yelling at laypersons? Scaring the shit out of them? That had been my experience with the FBI's "rapport-building interviewing technique."

"So now we've got a 302, and we don't know what's in it," Rob said.

Rob and Scott went back and forth with each other about statutes and codes and sections, 666s and 1343s and 7201s. It sounded like a foreign language. I rubbed my face with both hands. My eyes felt like they had cinders in them. I hadn't showered or shaved. I was wrecked. We'd been at this for six hours.

Rob must have seen my distress.

"Look, let's forget about a proffer," he said. "I wouldn't put you in front of the US Attorney right now. So let's table that. I can tell you're exhausted."

"He didn't sleep at all on the plane," my father said.

"Why is this case even in Boston?" I asked.

"Here's what I know," Rob said. "About a year ago, prosecutors here were working on something else—a securities fraud case—when their suspect said he had some information they might find interesting. He was looking for leniency. He said he knew of a college coach who'd taken bribes for recruiting spots. And that tip eventually led them to Singer.

"So, that allows the Boston prosecutors to manufacture jurisdiction through having their cooperators commit some of the criminal acts with a Massachusetts nexus."

The legalese hurt my head.

"You mean since it started here, it stays here?" I asked.

"Basically, yes."

Rob looked at his phone.

"Okay, they're ready. Scott and I will go over and see what we can do."

They left to make the three-block walk to the courthouse. My father and I sat without talking. I shivered. My father sipped water and I drank a Coke. We stared at the harbor. I wrung my hands and picked at my cuticles. My father crossed his legs. Minutes clicked by. Finally, my cell phone rang. I put Rob on speaker.

"So, listen. This thing is bigger than we thought. They have a podium set up, and I think the US Attorney General himself might be coming to announce whatever this is. It's big.

"But we worked on your deal, and we got it down to eighteen months. And they agreed not to pound the fist—meaning they're not going to be overly aggressive when we get to court. All right? So, this is it. You would be pleading guilty to a racketeering conspiracy charge."

"Racketeering?" I said with alarm, looking over at my father. He raised his eyebrows.

"Yes, it's actually a lesser charge. It's still a felony. They wouldn't go for a misdemeanor. But there's a chance you get off with just probation. That's not up to the prosecution. That will be up to the judge.

"Now we can certainly fight it, but that means you'd be coming back to Boston for a hearing, and that's not going to happen right away. It could be a year away. And since it's a racketeering charge, that means that all the coaches involved would be tried as a group."

"We'd be tried together? Even if I don't know them?"

"That's how racketeering charges work. It's not one-on-one. The jury hears evidence about everyone who's charged. And the other schools involved will probably have different admissions systems and different recruiting policies, so it's going to get complicated. The jury will have to listen to all of it and somehow decide that you're not like everyone else.

"I'm betting that these other guys are not innocent because they're not being offered a deal. And if any of these people have money, they'll delay it like crazy. If it was just you, we could go in and do the trial in like four days, maybe a year from now, and you'd be done. But it's racketeering, and that makes it much harder. You understand?"

"Yes," I said.

"I'm pretty confident you're the least culpable in all of this, with the least number of charges. The lawyers with the clients who have the most charges will do the majority of the talking. And there'll be lots of motions, a mountain of paperwork, and even though 99 percent of it won't pertain to you, I'm going to have to read through everything in case there's something in there that can help us. It's going to be a long, drawn-out process. You most likely won't be able to work. You'll be away from your family. You'll be in Boston going to court every day. And it's going to cost you a lot of money. I think probably a million and a half, two million."

I shot a look at my dad to register my shock.

"And if you win, you don't get that money back, and you probably won't have your job," Rob went on. "That's what winning looks like. So, it's up to you. If you want to defend yourself, I'm happy to do it. We'll go in and fight for you. But my fear is that we're going to be sitting in the courtroom and we'll be in the middle of month three of the trial, and things will not be looking great, and you're going to look at me and say, 'I should have taken that deal.'"

"What about the handbook? Did you show them that part about helping the team?" I asked.

"They said they didn't care about it."

"Well, before I do anything, I'd really like to talk to Stanford—"

"John, Stanford doesn't care about you. They want to sell you down the river as fast as they possibly can. They want this deal to happen. They get to save face, to say *they* were duped. And then they'll move on."

"That's such—"

"Unfortunately, I need to know now if you want to take the deal. They aren't going to let us leave without your decision. We have five minutes to make this happen."

I told Rob I'd call him right back. I had to talk to Molly. When she picked up, I put her on speaker and told her my father was there with me.

My dad jumped in. "Molly, I want to tell you how great John has been."

"Okay, well—"

"He's really just been terrific—and he didn't do this."

"I know that," she said. I could hear that she was irritated.

"Molly, listen to me," I said. "I only have a few minutes to tell you what the options are here."

I laid out what Rob had explained to me.

"We obviously don't have the money to fight this. Pleading guilty is my best chance of not going to jail. I'll be a felon, but then it's done."

"This is crazy," she said. "You would plead guilty to something you didn't do? That's actually what your lawyer is saying you should do?"

"He thinks it's my best option. Our best option. It's very complicated, but, yes, he thinks this is the way to go."

There was silence on her end.

"My career as a college coach is over," I went on. "But I'll just, I'll find something else. So, I plead guilty today, and then I can come home."

"God, this is just—"

"I know."

I waited.

"All right," she said softly. I could tell she was trying not to cry. "Yes?"

"Yes."

I felt surprisingly calm. Later, I would understand that I was probably in shock.

I called Rob back. "I'm going to do it."

"I think that's a good decision. Let me tell them."

About thirty minutes later, Scott and Rob returned to the conference room.

"The prosecution is happy to have you out of this. It's a cleaner case for them now," Rob said. "But they still get to say Stanford was involved."

He sat down next to me. "Now, I want to go over with you what it means to be a felon."

I couldn't believe he was talking about me, that I was that felon. I was a sailing coach.

"You can't own a gun. You can't vote, at least not in California. You won't be able to sit on most boards. But there are lots of jobs out there you can get."

He told me the finance world was one option; it was especially forgiving of white-collar criminals.

"I have a friend who was caught up in the 2008 banking scandal, and he went to jail, and he's back to living his life, working in finance again," he said. "You're the least culpable in this. People will see that."

I wasn't so sure. How would anyone see that? Plus, I was over forty. Was I really going to start a new career at my age?

"And you'll probably be able to coach again somewhere. Look at the Duke lacrosse coach," Rob said, referring to the coach who'd been forced to resign amidst a scandal. "He's building his career back up. People move on, and you'll be able to do that."

"I just can't believe this," I said. "How was I so stupid to let this happen?"

"Look, most *lawyers* don't even know these laws. I know plenty of nonlawyers would probably have done what you did. They would have had no idea that there was even a chance that it was illegal. There are so many gray areas in racketeering. The laws were written that way, to be broad. That's how the US Attorney's Office got Whitey Bulger."

I grunted. Now I was being lumped in with Boston's most notorious mobster. In 2013, when Rob was still in the US Attorney's Office, James "Whitey" Bulger had been convicted of thirty-one counts, including racketeering and participation in eleven murders. In the next several weeks, I would learn more than I ever cared to know about the Racketeer Influenced and Corrupt Organizations (RICO) law, which was passed in 1970 as a way to fight organized crime. Racketeering is not a specific crime—it's a catchall, a way of prosecuting thirty-five different offenses, including kidnapping, murder, arson, bribery, and mail and wire fraud. To be charged under RICO, you have to have allegedly committed at least two of those crimes within ten years.

Before RICO, the government could go after defendants charged with mob-related crimes only individually, which made it hard to shut down entire organizations. With the new law, prosecutors could indict everyone—the boss, the hitmen, the drivers, the girlfriends—and they would be tried en masse. RICO allowed the prosecution to threaten small-fish members with heavier sentences to pressure them into flipping on their higher-ups. But in the case I was caught up in, the law was being used backward: Rick Singer, the kingpin, was helping the government take down everyone beneath him. It seemed absurd.

Rob was still talking, but I had stopped listening. I was exhausted. I was numb. I had just agreed to say I was guilty of a federal crime. Everything I had ever thought about the justice system had been turned upside down. I had assumed that if you pleaded guilty, then you were, in fact, guilty. It was black and white. It never occurred to me that anyone would have a compelling reason to confess to doing something he or she hadn't done.

I learned later that plea bargaining dominates the justice system. More than 90 percent of people charged with federal crimes plead guilty, according to a 2018 study by the Pew Research Center—and most of them take plea deals. Of the 2 percent who actually go to trial, fewer than 1 percent win their cases.

The incentive to plead guilty comes largely, as it did for me, from the understanding that your punishment will be much worse if you go to trial and lose than if you take the deal the prosecution offers. Critics say this "trial penalty" encroaches on the Constitution's Sixth Amendment right to trial and has the effect of making it a rational choice to plead guilty to something you didn't do. This was how the system worked: innocence didn't matter.

MY FATHER AND I WALKED TO the car in silence, then I stared out the window as we took one wrong turn after another, trying to get out of Boston. When we finally found the Southeast Expressway, it was clogged with commuter traffic. My father suggested we call my mother to say we were on our way, and to tell her what I had just agreed to.

"Those goddamn assholes," she said when I told her the prosecutors had given me five minutes to decide whether I would plead guilty. I had to smile. I could always count on my mother to give voice to what was in my head.

Two hours later, we finally crossed the Sagamore Bridge spanning the Cape Cod Canal. When we got home, I talked to my mother briefly and then went up to my childhood room. From my bed, I could see a bookcase that still held a few of my old sailing trophies, as well as some geology and art history college textbooks. On another shelf was my collection of *Swallows and Amazons* books, magical stories written in the 1930s and 1940s about children having adventures in sailboats in the Lake District of England. I planned to read them to my kids someday.

I closed my eyes. I heard the wind moving through the trees, and I pictured the lake, dark and choppy and cold. I breathed in and out, deliberately and slowly, and then I was on that lake, alone in a small boat, and its sail was full and ghostly under an alabaster moon.

13

I was back home when Rob emailed me the prosecution's twelve-page Information document and the plea agreement I was to sign. He told me to read it over and call with questions. I had many.

"This isn't right," I said during one of our calls. "'In or about May 2018, after Stanford Applicant 1 deferred his application to Stanford for one year, Singer mailed a payment of $110,000 from one of the KWF charitable accounts to the Stanford sailing program in exchange for Vandemoer's agreement to designate Stanford Applicant 1 as a sailing recruit in the following year's recruitment cycle.' Applicant 1 is Bodhi, right?"

"Right," Rob said. "Bodhi."

"Singer is lying. That money wasn't in exchange for anything. He said no strings attached."

"We should assume that he's lying to them about some of these things," Rob said. "We could argue about the $110,000, but it wouldn't change anything for sentencing purposes. There's no point in fighting that. They're not letting go of it."

Later that day, Rob called to say he'd learned that more coaches were involved than he'd first thought. His guess was that I was still the only one being offered a deal by the prosecution.

"Why just me?" I said. "I don't understand."

"They're not doing it to be nice guys. They're doing it because they want you out of this. You hurt their case because you're different from the others. You didn't take any money for yourself. When I was in that office, you were the kind of person we feared most—someone who would muddy the waters."

"Why not let me go, then? Just drop it."

"They want the Stanford name in this," Rob said.

"This is so unfair, I—"

"We can get out now if you want to, you know," Rob said. "We haven't signed anything yet."

I said I would stick with my decision.

Rob told me in another call that he'd heard some parents were going to be charged, as well. "They seem very interested in Molly Zhao's family. Do you remember anything else about them? Anything that could be useful?"

I thought hard but could come up with nothing. I'd had no encounters with them. They had talked about coming for a tour, but it never happened. All the communication with them had been through Singer.

"I don't know anything about them. I have no idea why they donated that money. It doesn't make sense. She didn't even want to sail."

"Singer's a con artist," Rob said. "He gave you that money to make you feel comfortable with him, to gain your trust. He was grooming you. Predators do that."

On Sunday evening, after the kids were in bed, I sat down at the kitchen table with the document in front of me. Molly was finishing the dishes.

"So I have that Information thing," I said. "I read it all, and I'm going to sign it."

"Well, I haven't read it," Molly said, drying her hands on a towel. "We haven't even talked about it."

I knew I'd done a terrible job of keeping her informed. I think a part of me believed that if Molly and I didn't talk about it, it wasn't really happening. But seeing her pained face, I realized that I'd been wrong to shut her out. If we were going to get through this, we had to do it together. I asked her to sit with me at the kitchen table.

"How about you read it and then we'll talk it over," I said.

When she was done, she put the agreement down and looked at me. "I don't understand why you would sign this. You said this stuff isn't true."

For the next hour, I recounted what Rob had told me; how hard and expensive and likely futile it would be to fight, how my case would be drowned out in a group RICO trial, how pleading guilty would at least give me a shot at keeping our family together.

"But you're signing a document that says you're a liar."

"I know. It's insane. And I feel like I'm lying when I sign it. It's a fucked-up system. We're screwed no matter what we do."

Late that night, we both agreed I had no choice. I signed the document and emailed it to Rob. In the morning, he told me that the Information would be put under seal, and no one knew when it would be unsealed.

"They won't unseal it until they raid everyone involved," he said. "Otherwise, it would tip people off. The parents I've heard about are very wealthy, and the government is afraid they'll leave the country. Plus, they want the drama of doing the raid and dragging everyone in front of the court."

He said that as soon as it was unsealed, I would have to fly back to Boston to plead guilty in front of a judge.

"You should expect to be fired on that day," he said. "I'm pretty sure the government has coordinated the timing with Stanford, so they don't fire you prematurely and tip everyone off."

The humiliation was almost unbearable. Stanford had been communicating with the prosecution about the right time to dump me. They'd made up their mind about me without ever hearing my side of the story. And it was all to protect their image.

My job now was to live as if nothing was different, even though I was sitting on a ticking bomb that could not be defused. I didn't know when it would happen, but I knew I was about to lose everything: my team, my career, my reputation. Our primary source of income would be gone, as would our housing and our health insurance.

I went through the motions at practice. From the coach boat, I watched the players do drills. I offered advice. I did chalk talks at the whiteboard. I read through the players' daily surveys to see how they were feeling. I did my job. But all I could think about was what was going to happen to the team once the news broke. I wondered whether they would ever speak to me again and, more important, whether there was any way I could protect them from the shitstorm that I felt sure was going to hit them. I was sick that I was letting them and their families down. I'd sat in their living rooms when I recruited them and told their parents they could count on me. I'd watch out for their kids. I'd keep them safe. And now I'd completely failed them.

When I wasn't on the water, I fantasized about what I would say to Stanford administrators if I could get them to hear me out. Twice, I actually approached Patrick Dunkley's office thinking I would tell him everything, and he would understand and get Stanford to come to my defense. Twice, after greeting his assistant outside his door, I turned back, chiding myself first for not having the balls to go in there, and then for being stupid enough to think I could change anything by talking to him.

On Wednesday, March 6, Rob called to tell me he'd heard the documents would be unsealed the following Tuesday. "So, you should get out here on the eleventh."

I said I'd be there.

"And listen, there may be some media attention around this, but I wouldn't worry about it. If anything, you'll be a quick mention in the last paragraph of an ESPN story. It won't be a big deal for you," Rob said.

Now I knew when my career would end. March 12, 2019. I had six days to prepare to hand the reigns over to Clinton and Belle.

A few hours after my conversation with Rob, we had our usual team meeting in a conference room in the athletics building. I sat on a desk near the door and let Clinton do the talking. He went over the plans for the two big regattas we had coming up that weekend. He also spoke about the pair of sports performance consultants who'd observed our practices that week. I'd hired them using some of Rick Singer's donated money to assess how we functioned as a team and to make recommendations about how to improve. I'd been excited to have them there. Now I realized I'd never see their report and never get to implement their suggestions.

I scanned the team members' hopeful, smiling, open, trusting faces. It killed me that they were sitting there with no clue about what was going to happen. When the meeting broke up, I went to my office, sat at my desk, and waited. I shuffled papers. I tapped a pen. I bounced my knee. One by one, my fellow coaches took off for the day, calling out "Later!" and "Have a good night" as they walked by my open door.

When I was sure I was the only one left in the varsity suite, I loaded my things into cardboard boxes. I left a notebook and a two-tiered file holder on my desk and a few books on my bookshelf so it wouldn't be obvious I had vacated the place. While I packed, I rehearsed what I was going to say to Clinton and Belle. I knew I had to tell them. There was no way I would let them hear it from anyone but me. I owed them that.

Before practice the next day, I asked them to come up to the office space on the second floor of the boathouse. We sat in rolling chairs a few feet apart from each other.

"So, I—some, some big things have happened," I said. "And so the end result is, what's going to happen, I'll explain it all to you in a minute, but what's going to happen is I'm going to be fired next week."

"What?" Clinton said. Belle's mouth fell open.

I told them about Rick Singer and the donations and the charges that had been brought against me. "I didn't intend for any of this to happen. I didn't realize what he was doing. But I can't fight it. I don't have the money to do that. And my lawyer said that with the evidence they have, everything Singer told them, even though a lot of it is lies, it would be really tough."

"This can't just be it," Clinton said. "Can't we do something?"

Belle looked at the floor. I felt for her. She had just graduated from college. This was her first coaching job, and now she had to deal with this.

"I can't stop it from happening. Stanford knows all about it, and they're going to fire me. So, what I want you to know is that I shared a Google Drive with you guys. It has all the travel plans, everything for spring break, all the regatta stuff. And all the recruiting information. It should be everything you need."

Then I handed Clinton the keys to my campus office.

"You guys run practice today. I'm not going to go out on the water."

"I'm so sorry, man," Clinton said. "This just sucks."

The team arrived and got busy rigging the boats. Once they had launched, I started to pack my car, which I'd parked on the far side of the boathouse where I knew it wouldn't be visible from the water. I tied my two stand-up paddleboards on top of my car and hauled out box after box.

When I saw the boats coming back in, I went down to meet them on the dock. Then we did what we always did on the Thursday before regattas; we gathered just inside the open bay door to talk about the upcoming weekend.

"This will be our first big opportunity to see lots of competition," I said, facing them. "We'll get to compare ourselves to other teams— especially the ones coming off early spring break. They will have had a lot of time on the water. So, in the team race, our goal should be to make it to the final four, to get in all the racing we can. And for the women going to Navy, this is a great—"

My words caught in my throat. I fought to regain my composure. *Don't let them see it. They can't see it.* I forced myself to go on. When I was done, we wrapped things up as we always did, by forming a circle and putting our hands in the middle. Then we all shouted, "One team! One plan! One goal! One Stanford!"

The players gathered up their gear. They were talking and laughing and calling out their good-byes. I watched them walk away, admiring them and feeling proud of them and hoping and praying that when this all came to light, they would be okay. They were amazing kids. Smart and funny and engaged. They had pushed me to be better. I wanted to know who they would become when they went out into the world. I knew they would do spectacular things. I also knew that after this weekend, I'd probably never see most of them again.

I walked outside and stood at the top of the ramp that led down to the docks. The sun had dropped behind the Santa Cruz Mountains and left the sky banded with pink and orange. The unruffled creek mirrored the intense colors. The boats were lined up neatly on the dock, buttoned up for the night. I'd always loved that sight. I heard the whine of a motorboat in the distance. I breathed in the familiar marshy air.

"Hey," Clinton called to me.

I turned to face him. "Heading out?"

"Yeah. See you this weekend."

"See you," I said.

I went back into the boathouse and walked around one last time, telling myself I was checking to see whether I'd left anything behind. But really, I just wanted to hold on to it all for a few more minutes—the whiteboard with the players' goals written on it, and the rack of rolled sails, and the neat coils of nylon line. I looked up at the orange racing marks hanging from the staircase banister and, for the last time, gazed at the three white banners attached to a second-floor railing. On them, in black lettering, were all the conference championships Stanford had ever won. Most of them had been under my watch. But what did it matter now?

I went upstairs, turned out the lights, and used an Allen wrench to lock the crash bar on the door that led to the exterior stairs. Then I walked out and let the heavy door slam behind me.

14

On Friday, March 8, I left the house at 4 a.m. to pick up Belle and the women who were racing that weekend at Navy. When we landed in Baltimore, I said goodbye to them and rented a car. I planned to drive eighty-five miles south to St. Mary's College to rendezvous with Clinton and the group that was competing there. By the time I got on the road, it was raining and dark and cold. My GPS told me there were accidents on the main highway, so it rerouted me, and then, because of more bad traffic ahead, it rerouted me again, this time onto a two-lane back road. I'd made the trip to St. Mary's countless times, but I had no idea where I was. Nothing looked familiar.

I wondered whether I'd made a mistake. Was I heading north? I searched for roadside signs and saw none. My windows were fogging up, and I twisted several dials on the dashboard trying to find the defroster. A pair of oncoming headlights seemed to be veering into my lane. Now frozen pellets were mixing in with the rain and pinging off the car. I checked the gauge and saw the outside temperature had dropped to thirty-four degrees. Shit. Gripping the steering wheel tighter, I strained to see through the slapping windshield wipers whether the sheen on the pavement was water or black ice. I had a vision of my car careening off the road and plunging into the dark forest. No one would know what had happened to me. I'd never be found. Maybe that wouldn't be the worst thing.

I drove on, muttering to myself, cursing the sleet and the dark road and goddamn Rick Singer until the GPS, at last, routed me back to the highway. I arrived at the Fairfield Inn in Lexington Park, where Clinton and the other players had already checked in. I was shaky and spent, but I knew there was no chance I'd be able to get right to sleep. I watched college basketball for hours and then a movie, and finally drifted off around 3 a.m.

Five hours later, with an icy fog starting to lift, the team, Clinton, and I headed for the college sailing center on the edge of the compact, green campus. The two-story brick and clapboard building had a columned front porch overlooking a broad bend in the tidal St. Mary's River, where the racing would take place. I had always loved coming here for regattas. It took me back to a happy, simpler time in my life when I'd been assisting Adam Werblow, and when I'd first met Molly. Now, I almost couldn't bear to see it.

I'd texted Adam to say I wanted to talk to him alone if he had a minute. I'd done the same with John Morgan, the president of the Club 420 Association, who I knew would be there to watch his son sail for Hobart. I'd also asked Clinton to act as head coach that day. I said I'd fly the drone and check in down on the docks during race rotations.

After wishing the team good luck, I climbed up a low hill that was still covered in frost and followed a trail several hundred yards to an old graveyard on a treeless knoll. I'd often stood up there for races; it offered an unobstructed view of the racecourse and was ideal for flying drones. Plus, I usually had it to myself. I liked to watch races alone so I could concentrate. I stamped my feet, blew on my hands, and tried to focus on getting the drone up. Instead, a string of words ran through my head like a sad mantra: *This is where my career began, and this is where it will end.*

Before lunchtime, I saw John Morgan coming up the trail. He was such a good friend and I looked up to him so much. How was I going to tell him?

"Thought I'd find you up here," he said. "How's it going?"

"Well . . . ," I said and launched into my story.

His face registered his shock.

"Stanford is going to fire me, probably Tuesday. And they're testifying against me."

"This is unbelievable. I'm so, so sorry," he said, shaking his head. "This shouldn't be happening to you. Universities are big businesses. They shouldn't be, but they are."

John offered to help me find new lawyers if I needed them. "And I'll do everything I can to help you keep your job with the association."

Maybe if the whole thing blew over quickly, he said, I'd be okay. I thanked him, but I think we both knew that there was little chance the board would let me stay on once this news got out.

I SPENT SATURDAY NIGHT IN MY hotel room, searching online for bribery cases that might somehow relate to mine. I knew the internet was not my friend—browsing legal proceedings was almost as counterproductive and as terrifying as researching medical symptoms—but I couldn't stop. One case kept popping up, and the more I read about it, the angrier I got. In October 2018, Jerome Allen, an assistant Boston Celtics coach and the former UPenn head basketball coach, had pleaded guilty to money laundering for accepting an $18,000 bribe from the parent of a prospective UPenn student-athlete. Allen had been ordered to pay a $202,000 fine. The Celtics suspended him for two weeks but kept him on their roster.

At the time, Celtics general manager Danny Ainge told *The Boston Globe*, "I'm disappointed that this happened, but I've also been very impressed with how [Allen's] owned up, taken full responsibility for it, and hasn't fallen into the line of thinking that, 'This is the world of college basketball,' or anything like that. . . . He holds himself to a high standard and took immediate responsibility for it right out of the gate."

How was this fair? Jerome Allen only had to pay a fine, and he was still working with the NBA? And getting compliments from his boss? I fired off a rambling email to Rob Fisher.

"I'm really struggling with how bad my punishment is. I took no money. I didn't even support these kids into school, they didn't even apply and I'm a felon for the rest of my life and I may go to jail. The NBA isn't going to hire me, there is nothing like that for my sport. My career has ended. Doesn't the Allen case draw some sort of floor for this? A wealthy donor gives him tens of thousands of dollars to get his kid into school, and he does, and his kid is still in school and doesn't play on the team. What am I missing?"

I stewed about the Jerome Allen case and my plea agreement into the early morning hours. This was absolute bullshit. What was I doing, rolling over like this? I should stand up for myself. Maybe I was getting bad advice. I should get out of the plea deal, fight this thing.

On Sunday morning, the river was glass, and the start of the regatta was delayed. I was still riled up. I walked behind the sailing center and called Rob.

"Jerome Allen's case is different from yours," he said. "He's cooperating. His punishment is only being delayed."

I was instantly deflated. Somehow I'd half-expected Rob to say,

Wow, John, this is just what we've needed. Fantastic research. Let me go back to the prosecution and get your charge immediately reduced to a misdemeanor.

"Really?" I said. "Because I thought his case was very similar, with his plea and all that. Like maybe it established some precedent or something." I was pacing and trying to keep my voice down. I lifted my chin a few times to greet coaches as they walked by. "I thought this might be a way, I don't know, to just—"

"You know we can back out of the deal if you don't feel comfortable," Rob said gently. "It's entirely up to you."

"Right."

"But it's going to be tough."

"I know."

At 2 a.m., I'd been almost sure I wanted to change my mind. Now, the reality of what it would cost me was once again depressingly clear. I told Rob I would stick with our plan.

After the call, I spotted Adam Werblow. I knew he was busy hosting the regatta, but the delay had given him a little downtime.

"Got a minute?"

"Sure, as long as the wind doesn't kick in," he said.

We went into his office and I told him what was going on.

"This can't be happening," he said. "I don't understand. How did you break the law?"

"Apparently, I did. They're saying I did."

"Can I do anything?"

"There's really nothing."

Adam's radio crackled with voices. The breeze was filling in from the south.

"Sorry," he said. "I've got to go."

"Me, too."

"Listen, John," he said as we both stood up. "We'll get you coaching again. Forget about Stanford. You're going to be okay. We'll get you going again."

I choked up as I tried to say thank you.

The racing got under way. Stanford battled Brown and Hobart for the top positions, and in the end, we came out victorious. I was very happy for the team and for Clinton. While I helped pack up, John Mollicone, the Brown coach and a good friend, came over to say congratulations and to talk about spring break. Our two teams had made plans to train together in Florida.

"Really looking forward to it," John said.

"Me, too," I said, forcing myself to smile. "It's going to be great."

I felt like such an asshole lying to him.

I walked with Clinton and the players to the parking lot near the boathouse and watched as they loaded into their rented Suburban for the drive back to the airport. I knew that when I said goodbye to these players—Wiley and Jack and Jacob, Meg, Taylor, and Kathryn—that I was probably saying goodbye forever. I had no idea how they would react when they heard the news, how they would think about me—and even more worrisome, how people would think about them. From behind the steering wheel, Clinton held my gaze for an extra beat and then said, "So long."

I couldn't get in my car just yet. I turned toward the river and started up a worn path. I knew where I was headed, to a secluded little waterside park called the Garden of Remembrance. I'd assembled the team there at the end of nationals in 2014 to say a tearful goodbye. They were my first recruiting class, and I had wanted them to know how proud I was and how much they meant to me.

I walked into the garden and sat down on a cold, wood-slat bench near a dry stone fountain and a gnarled tree strangled with vines. Then I put my hands over my face, bent over, and cried.

When I had pulled myself together enough to drive, I headed for the airport, where I was meeting up with Belle and the women's team. They hadn't had a great weekend, but by the time I joined them, they had already shifted their focus to upcoming exams. I kept to myself as we waited to board. When we landed, I drove everyone back to campus. I dropped a few of the players off right at their dorms; I didn't like them walking home alone late at night. And, as if it were any other weekend, I said, "See you soon. Good luck with your exams."

AT HOME, MOLLY WAS SITTING UP in bed, waiting for me. "Congrats on the win."

"Yeah, I was happy for them."

We managed to avoid acknowledging the harsh truth that in a just few hours, I had to get up and board a plane for Boston.

After breakfast the next morning, Molly and I talked out of earshot of the kids about the possibility that the FBI would be raiding some of our fellow coaches' homes early the following day. March 12—the day Rob said the government planned to descend on suspects' homes and make arrests. We had no idea if other Stanford coaches were involved in this thing.

"You think it will be loud?" Molly asked. "Like they'll be banging on doors and shouting?"

"I don't know. I just hope it will all be over quick," I said. "But maybe plan on leaving a little later tomorrow so the kids don't see anything scary."

I helped Molly get Nicholas and Nora into the stroller so she could walk them to daycare, then went inside to get my suitcase and loaded it into the car. As I started for the airport, I passed Molly and the kids. I tooted my horn.

"Daddyyyyyy!!!" Nicholas yelled, waving madly.

Molly lifted her hand and gave me a tight-lipped smile. I knew I would never forget the way their faces looked that morning.

15

'd stayed in the Residence Inn in Cambridge dozens of times over the years when my teams sailed against MIT, Harvard, and Boston University. The hotel was only half a mile from the Charles River Basin, the broad section of the river where the colleges have their boathouses and held regattas. It felt surreal to be back in that familiar hotel room putting on a suit and a tie, getting ready to go plead guilty to a federal crime.

I found my father waiting for me in the lobby. We were going to drive over to the courthouse together. My hearing wasn't until 3 p.m., but Rob wanted us to have plenty of time to get paperwork done.

"Rob left me a message," I said as I buckled my seat belt. "Rick Singer is going to be here, too. He said there could be some media attention, but they won't be there for me."

My dad flashed me a worried look.

We drove across the Longfellow Bridge. The Boston skyline was before us: the silvery Hancock and Prudential towers, the low red-brick townhouses of Beacon Hill, the bare trees along the Esplanade.

A puffy northwest wind, blowing twelve, maybe thirteen knots, was darkening patches of the basin. I knew that breeze well.

When we got to the Seaport, we parked in a garage and walked to the Moakley Courthouse, a contemporary brick building with a five-story conical glass wall that faces the harbor.

No one knows what I'm about to do, I kept thinking as we passed people on the sidewalk. *No one knows what is about to happen to me.*

Inside the arched main entrance was an airy rotunda. Rob Fisher was waiting for us. After my father and I turned in our cell phones at a security desk, we all climbed a granite staircase to a café in a mul-tistory atrium that had views of the water. We took seats at a small table. I had my back to the harbor.

"So," Rob said, folding his hands together. "We're ready?"

My chest tightened.

"I don't know," I said. I pulled at my shirt collar.

Rob gave me a sympathetic smile.

"I'm pleading guilty to something I didn't do," I said.

"You know we can fight it."

"No," I said. I looked over at my father. "I don't know."

"We'll rip up the plea agreement right now. But it will be an uphill battle. They'll come at you hard."

I nodded and chewed at my thumbnail.

"We're going to have to explain everything—the texts and the emails, all of it—and everything will be presented out of context. And it will come down to whether the jury believes you or Singer. And I have to tell you, juries almost always believe the government witness, even if they know the guy did bad things."

"It doesn't seem right."

"This is where we are. You can start over. But you have to choose right now."

My instinct was to fight, to not roll over—and to not lie. But I had to put my family first, and the best thing, the only thing, for them was to see through what I had started.

"Okay."

"Yes?"

"Yes," I said. "I'll do it."

Just then, I noticed two men and a woman standing about a hundred feet away near the elevator bank. One of them stood out. There was no mistaking that hair and that reptilian smile. It was Rick Singer.

I stiffened. "There he is right there."

My dad turned to look.

"Singer," I said.

"That's him?"

"That's him." I wanted to jump up and lunge at him, to put my hands around his neck.

"He's pleading just before you today," Rob said. "Same courtroom."

I couldn't take my eyes off him.

"John."

How could he look so calm, so relaxed?

"John."

I snapped my attention back to Rob.

"I was saying we should go check in with the probation officer and the US Marshals office. If we get that done ahead of time, then after you plead, you can just leave."

We got up and went in the opposite direction from Singer and then walked back down the stairs to the ground level.

"So, you lucked out and got Martha Victoria for a pretrial probation officer," Rob said as we walked. "She's really good. She'll be the one reporting to the judge."

I had no idea what that meant, but I was glad he thought it was a good thing. Rob and I went into the probation office. Martha Victoria was pleasant enough as she asked me a series of questions—*What would your high school classmates say about you? Was I under psychiatric care? How much debt was I carrying?*—but I sensed that she could quickly turn steely if I did anything other than answer succinctly.

At around 11:30, after we'd been in her office for nearly an hour, Rob looked at his phone.

"Okay, it just hit. They're doing the press conference upstairs right now," he said. His eyes got big. "Oh, wow. This thing is—. Wow. This is enormous."

He looked up. "Sorry, Martha. I'll wait until we're finished here."

Rob and I hurried out to the hall when I was done and found my dad sitting on a bench near the stairway.

"They're announcing everything now," I said.

Rob was looking at his phone. "Scott sent me the indictment. This is way, *way* bigger than we thought. Fifty people. Thirty-three parents, nine coaches. Exam proctors. Wow. Two actresses. Felicity Huffman. Lori Loughlin. Oh my god. Gordon Caplan at the law firm Willkie. There's cheating on college entrance exams, the SAT and the ACT."

"What?" I said. "Cheating on tests? Who?"

Rob scrolled with his thumb. "Parents paid between $15,000 and $75,000 to have someone either take the exam for their child or to correct their child's answers afterward—"

"Are you serious? That's disgusting," I said. "Singer did that?"

I had never heard anything about tests. I had nothing to do with that. I was horrified that my name would forever be attached to these cheaters.

Rob kept reading. "Parents paid Singer $25 million to bribe coaches and university administrators."

"Are there other Stanford coaches?"

"No. I don't think so. USC, UCLA, Yale, Georgetown, Wake Forest, University of Texas, University of San Diego. No other Stanford. They might not be done, though."

I was stunned. Just me?

Rob said he'd walk with me to the Marshals office where I would be fingerprinted and have my mug shot taken. We went down a dingy, mustard-yellow hallway lined with framed posters from *The Fugitive* and *U.S. Marshals* and other movies of that ilk. Rob went to a window to check me in. In a moment, a buzzer sounded, and a beefy guy wearing a T-shirt, jeans, and a holstered gun came through a door.

"Vanda-moah," he barked.

"You want me to come?" Rob asked the officer.

"No, just him."

I followed the man through two sets of doors that opened only when he looked up at the cameras mounted above them. At the end of the hall, he ushered me into a small room with cement floors and exposed brick walls and pipes, so bleak it looked like it once might have been a boiler room. Behind a long desk, three poker-faced marshals in coats and ties were looking up at a mounted television that had the picture on without sound. The US Attorney's press briefing was on. I felt like I was both watching and starring in a horror movie.

"Fingers there," said the man who had brought me in, indicating a device on the desk. I put my shaking hand on the screen.

"No," he said. "There."

I tried again.

"Fingers. No," he said sharply.

I pressed them down once more.

"Okay, stand there." He pointed to a makeshift white screen. I stood in front of it, and he took my picture.

I waited awkwardly in the middle of the room while the agent typed using only his two index fingers. The other marshals shot looks my way and then went back to the TV screen. I felt like a criminal.

When he was finished with me, the marshal walked me back out. Something went wrong with the automatic doors, and he had to yell into his walkie-talkie to get them to open. Finally, I rejoined my father and Rob.

"What do you want to do now?" Rob asked. "We've got a few hours."

"Walk? I don't know. Get lunch, maybe."

"Sure. Listen, when you go outside, there may be some reporters. They might not recognize you yet, but if they do, say nothing. Just keep walking. They'll break off from you eventually. I'll meet you back here."

My father and I went down to the lobby, retrieved our phones, and went through the glass courthouse doors to the sidewalk. Immediately, several reporters surrounded us, yelling, "How do you know Rick Singer?" and "Why did you do this?" as they followed us down the street. How did they even know who I was? Why did they care? A cameraman ran just ahead of us and then turned around and walked backward, shooting video. I heard rapid-fire shutter bursts of still cameras at my side. I didn't know where to look.

"Why did you do this, John?" A reporter yelled again. We turned toward the water and the pack followed us for another block before dropping back.

At the Barking Crab, a clam shack restaurant fronting an empty marina, I ordered a fish sandwich and a Coke, then picked up my phone to check my email. And there it was. Stanford had wasted no time. Patrick Dunkley had written to "inform me that I was being fired with cause." I'd been expecting it, but it was a shock to see it in writing.

"Well, Stanford just fired me."

My father rested his hand on my forearm. "I'm sorry."

When the sandwich arrived, I took one bite and put it down. I couldn't eat.

"That's okay," my dad said. I sipped my Coke and chewed on the straw while my father ate his lunch.

When we walked back toward the courthouse, we could see reporters coming for us.

"Hold your head high," my dad said. "You have nothing to be ashamed of."

There were more of them now, and they were more aggressive, surrounding us and pushing cameras at our faces and shouting, "Any comment?" As much as I dreaded what was to come, it was a relief to get back into the relative shelter of the courthouse. Rob spotted us, and together, we got on an elevator.

"So, some good news," Rob said. "Prosecutor Andrew Lelling said during the Q&A there was one coach who didn't take any money for himself. He didn't mention you by name. But we can work with that in the hearing."

At the fifth floor, we stepped out into a tide of people heading for Courtroom 12, where Rick Singer was about to appear. Rob and Scott had said they were going to sit in on his hearing. They'd come out and find us when it was getting close to wrapping up.

My father and I found a bench facing the sloped glass wall at the far end of the curved open corridor. We were out of the fray but still had a view of the courtroom door. We watched the steady stream of men and women in business attire and reporters in jeans and down jackets disappear into the courtroom.

"Dad. Look."

Singer had appeared. In a dark suit, with a blue parka over one arm, he looked at ease, as if he were heading for drinks with colleagues. He laughed when one of the men he was with—I assumed it was a lawyer—leaned toward him and spoke. They made their way through the cluster of reporters and onlookers and entered the courtroom.

Rob had said Singer's hearing would take about half an hour. As the minutes ticked by, I stewed about what I could have done differently. I could have gone to someone right away, a higher-up at Stanford, when I first heard about the Zhao family donation. I could have said, "This seems a little weird and gray and I want to make sure it's fine." I could have told Rick Singer to get lost. I could have stopped taking his calls.

I could have asked more questions. But wait, how would I have even known to ask more questions? Had Stanford ever once talked to me about what to do if I was presented with an unusual donation? No. I had assumed that the university thoroughly vetted all gifts. That was not my job.

Still, how could I have been blind to what Singer was doing? Or had I seen it—and chosen to look the other way? No. That wasn't it. I'd been naïve. I'd been tricked. I was such a fool, letting myself be flattered and played. Jesus, I'd handed my whole life to Rick Singer.

Forty minutes later, the courtroom doors remained closed, and I was still silently pummeling myself.

"Let's walk a little," my dad said. We went past a few courtroom entrances and then over to a railing to look down at the café several floors below us. Beyond the glass curtain was a small waterfront park and the wind-churned harbor. I spotted the South Shore commuter ferry pulling away from the dock at Rowes Wharf. I felt a bone-deep desire to be on that boat.

I heard Rob's voice behind me. "He's still going."

He joined us at the railing. "This guy just won't stop. He's really going to work on the judge. It's incredible. But I see what you saw, John. He's got a lot of charisma."

I would read later in the court transcript how Singer had stayed very still while he sat at the defense table and pleaded guilty to rack-eteering conspiracy and three other charges that carried a maximum sentence of sixty-five years. And when it was his turn to speak, he had acknowledged his crimes in much more detail than what prosecutor Eric Rosen had presented. Yes, your honor, he had said, he had indeed laundered money through his foundation and obstructed justice by warning six families he was wearing a wire and managed all the moving parts of the elaborate scheme to cheat on college entrance exams. And, yes, he'd targeted coaches and administrators who would take bribes in exchange for slotting his clients as recruited athletes.

Singer had explained his vision to the court. "So . . . there is a front door of getting in where a student just does it on their own; and then there's a back door, where people go to institutional advance-ment and they make large donations, but they're not guaranteed to get in. And then I created a side door that guaranteed families to get in. So that was what made it very attractive to so many families . . . I created a guarantee."

I wasn't aware of any of this at the time. All I knew was that I had somehow been sucked up into the Singer vortex and then dropped into this unfathomable ring of hell.

Scott joined us at the railing and said, "Time to go."

I was trembling as I followed him and Rob through the heavy wooden doors. We stepped first into a paneled antechamber and then into the open courtroom, where benches like church pews faced the judge's elevated oak perch and an oddly cheerful-looking stencil de-sign arced around the room. Rob gestured that we should sit on the bench in the last row. Reporters immediately slid in on either side and then filled the seats directly in front of us. Scott and Rob stood up and put their backs to some of them.

I looked past my lawyers and noticed a small group standing and talking near the empty jury box. I froze when I recognized one of the women; it was Elizabeth Keating, the IRS agent who had come to my house in February. She was beaming. And then, to the group's left, I spotted Rick Singer. He was half-sitting on the defense table with one foot on the ground and his other leg swinging freely. Martha Victoria was speaking with him while his lawyers packed up their briefcases. I was only half-hearing Rob as he gave me last-minute instructions. I was fixated on Singer.

"We can go up now," Scott said. We slid past the reporters. Rob pointed out where my father should sit, just behind the defense table. I walked through an opening in a low railing. Singer was now standing with his back to me. When we were only inches apart, he turned, and suddenly, we were face-to-face. I looked him in the eyes and clenched my fists. His face went pale and slack, and he looked down and away. Without lifting his head, he followed his lawyers up the aisle toward the exit.

I wanted to shout, "Why me? Why me, you asshole?"

But I knew why. He'd seen something in me—eagerness, naïveté, and a sorry yearning for validation. And he'd gone in for the kill.

16

told myself a two-part story about Singer. One was that I had been doing my job. The other was that I was so good at my job that he had been compelled to invest in me—in *my* program. But the truth was, I had no idea who the real Rick Singer was. It wasn't until the news broke and the media went deep in their hunt for Singer origin stories that I found out who I'd been dealing with.

People who remembered him in his North Side suburban Chicago hometown of Lincolnwood told the *Sacramento Bee* newspaper that he was hypercompetitive and aggressive even as a Little League pitcher. He was the league leader in both home runs and hit batsmen. At Niles West High School, in neighboring Skokie, he lettered in basketball and baseball. Still, he declared under his senior yearbook photo that he "would most like to be remembered for the outstanding personality I have been given, and being able to get along with others."

Although he would later tell a reporter he was a four-sport standout at Texas A&M, in truth, he bounced around from one small Texas college to another until finally graduating at age twenty-six from Trinity University in San Antonio, where he played only baseball and basketball. While he was a student, he also served as an assistant basketball coach at a local high school, but he was let go for berating players. Later, he falsely claimed he'd been the school's head coach for two years and led the team to the state championships' semifinals.

Singer moved to Sacramento in 1988 and started coaching basketball at both Sierra College and the Encina Preparatory High School. He was fired from the high school job, according to the *Bee*, when parents complained about his over-the-top sideline antics and abusive behavior toward officials. After earning a master's degree in school counseling from California's University of La Verne in 1992, Singer reinvented himself as a college counselor and life coach. His timing was excellent. The little-known field of independent education consulting was about to take off.

By 1994, when Singer started the business he named Future Stars, the notion that getting into a highly selective college or university was essential to future success and happiness had initiated its death grip on the American psyche. This fervor was fanned in part by the annual college ranking issue of *U.S. News & World Report*, which by then had become a best-selling stand-alone book, and the just-debuted "The Best 368 Colleges" from *The Princeton Review*, which rated top-twenty schools in a variety of categories. (Stanford would be consistently ranked the number one "dream school" for both students and parents.)

The rankings helped fire up acute admissions anxiety among students and parents. Meanwhile, the Common Application, a single form that students could submit to any participating school, went online in 1998. Now it was a breeze to apply to multiple colleges— including all eight Ivies and Stanford—even if the odds of being admitted were slim. The Common App limited students to a maximum of twenty applications, but kids reportedly found ways around that by creating multiple accounts. Some students were submitting thirty, forty, fifty, even seventy applications. More applications meant lower admittance rates. Lower rates boosted status—and status, of course, pulled in even more applications.

"Students and parents see the stories about how impossible admission has become, and in response submit more applications," wrote Jim Jump, a former president of the National Association for College Admission Counseling, in an online op-ed for *Inside Higher Ed.* "Colleges aren't sure which applications are serious, and in response place more students on waitlists. That leads to stories about how college admission is impossible, which starts the cycle all over again."

The hamster wheel reached warp speed in 2016 when *New York Times* columnist Frank Bruni wrote that Stanford's acceptance rate had plummeted to zero. "With no one admitted to the class of 2020, Stanford is assured that no other school can match its desirability in the near future."

Not all readers recognized it as an April Fool's joke.

Affluent parents, who were used to plowing difficulty and disappointment out of the way for their children, saw that the college admissions game was frighteningly out of their control. It was time to call in professionals. In Sacramento, that meant Rick Singer. Parents passed around his name on soccer game sidelines and at cocktail parties. He had the inside track, they said. He knew the right people. He could get the job done.

"Singer knew how to appeal to the panic of wealthy parents who fear that their children will not get into exclusive universities. He promised the certainty they craved," wrote journalists Daniel Golden and Doris Burke in *The New Yorker.*

Parents praised Singer's remarkable ability to get instant buy-in from their sulky teens. They also admired his supreme confidence. He promised clients he'd get their offspring into the school of their choice. It was a brazen guarantee that made other school counselors cringe—and parents swoon.

Dorothy Missler, a former high school counselor in Sacramento who met Singer some twenty years ago, told the *New York Times* that "he was like the Pied Piper. He played the music, and they followed him down the lane."

Singer briefly left college counseling in 2000 to work for West Corporation, a telemarketing firm in Omaha. Once settled there, he volunteered to coach a floundering middle school basketball team representing a Jewish community center.

According to the *Omaha World-Herald*, "His former players remember a dedicated coach who got them to play harder than they ever had. They also remember a lunatic on the sidelines, the Bobby Knight of middle school hoops, ranting at referees, rankling other coaches and eventually challenging a parent to a fistfight."

Singer built the team into one of the best in the league, and he seemed to have no compunction about proving it by running up scores against hapless opposing squads. He also appeared to be willing to cheat to gain an even bigger advantage. One former player told the sports blog Deadspin that he recalled Singer trying to bring in a tall, Catholic ringer to play on the team during a national tournament exclusively for Jewish athletes.

Singer moved back to Sacramento and returned to the counseling field with the launch of a placement service he called the CollegeSource. He shot for the moon with his advisory board and landed a handful of education bigwigs, including Ted Mitchell, then president of California's Occidental College.

"Rick has an encyclopedic knowledge of colleges and universities in America," Mitchell told the *Sacramento Business Journal* in 2005.

"Far more important, Rick is really great at getting at the heart of what kids and families want—and finding the right match."

Singer performed legitimate services for hundreds of apparently satisfied clients, including pro golfer Phil Mickelson and NFL Hall of Fame quarterback Joe Montana. But he also showed that he was willing to color outside the lines. Some parents reported that Singer had suggested their children beef up their applications by falsely claiming to be ethnic minorities or exaggerating their extracurricular activities.

In 2008, according to *The New Yorker*, Jon Reider, then director of college counseling at a top San Francisco high school and a former Stanford admissions officer, emailed Ted Mitchell, and other advisory board members, and urged them to stop working with Singer.

"Do you want to be associated with this guy?" he wrote. "He is the epitome of sleaze in the private counseling business."

Mitchell replied, "I strongly disagree . . . Do you know Rick? He's a decent guy, Jon, and I'd love to find a time to introduce the two of you."

Singer had ambitions beyond his counseling business. In 2010, he pitched a reality television show about what he called the "insane" business of dealing with overwrought families on the college hunt. Wearing a sporty sky-blue tennis vest and a white polo in his audition tape, he looked into the camera and said of the admissions process, "This is a game. Just realize that this is a game." He also cautioned parents that the stakes had changed in the old-school, legal practice of making large donations to give offspring a leg up when it came time for admissions decisions.

"At some schools giving $10 million isn't enough, because $10 million makes no impact on their school," Singer said. "They want $30, $40, $50 million . . ."

The audition may have been a bust, but Singer's star rose nonetheless. He was a popular speaker at financial firms and elite private schools. Audience members said they were won over by the track suit–clad counselor's energy, charm, and conviction. They believed him when he said he had the combination to the ever more befuddling padlock that was college admissions.

By 2011, when court documents show he began operating his scheme to cheat on college entrance exams, parents were lining up to pay as much as $15,000 a year for Singer's services. The following year, business was so good that he moved into a five-bedroom, $1.5 million Mediterranean-style house in tony Newport Beach, south of Los Angeles. He also set up the Key Worldwide Foundation, a charity purported to help underprivileged kids get into college.

Singer self-published two slim books in 2014: *Getting In: Gaining Admission to Your College of Choice*, and *Getting In, Personal Brands: A Personal Brand Is Essential to Gaining Admission to the College of Your Choice*. Both covers featured the same close-up picture of his face looking downright professorial in round wire-rim glasses. The books put forth his belief in doing whatever it takes to portray yourself as the person you want others to see—even if it is just an act.

Among his nuggets of advice:

"Whenever possible, believe your own story."

"When you're exhausted from trying to explain yourself to a world that wasn't made for people like you, remember your pitch. You are a vibrant and complex human being . . . and your pitch is what gets you in the door to live like it."

"Be confident. Act like you know what you're doing. Act like you belong. And if you can't do that, act like you're someone who can act like that."

"If you want people around you to support your brand, you have to make them believe it . . . Listen to their ideas, help them with their problems, feed their dreams."

"If you're presenting yourself as a reformed character who can show his or her scars with pride, think like that character. Be a method actor."

He also borrowed from Shakespeare, recalling when Hamlet marveled about his murderous uncle, Claudius: "That one may smile, and smile, and be a villain."

Singer cautioned: "Smilers are not your friends, your colleagues or your benefactors. Their agendas will hurt you sooner than you think."

As I read his words, I could only shake my head. Rick Singer seemed to be describing himself.

17

Scott, Rob, and I took seats at the defense table. Rob picked up a pitcher, poured three glasses of water, and then put his hand on my knee. "Doing okay?"

"Yes."

"If you have any questions, just ask. We can pause at any time. You don't need to say a lot."

Rob had told me the judge we'd been assigned, Rya Zobel, was generally more liberal than her Boston colleagues, but she tended to grill defendants who were pleading guilty. My job, he said, was to answer clearly and briefly. He had even sent me some transcripts of cases that had gone badly in front of her. He'd wanted me to see the consequences of straying from the simple script.

Judge Zobel entered the courtroom. She was a petite woman, in her eighties, with short, dyed-brown hair. A clerk at a low table in front of the bench spoke.

"This is *United States vs. John Vandemoer*, and it's Criminal 19-10079."

I cringed.

In a clipped German accent, Judge Zobel addressed me about my rights and then told me, "The only way we can proceed with something less than an indictment is if you agree to waive the indictment. Is that what you are planning to do?"

"Yes, that's what I plan to do," I said. I worried I hadn't spoken loudly enough.

"I understand that you are prepared to offer a plea of guilty to this one-count Information that charges you with racketeering conspiracy; is that correct?"

"Yes."

The judge looked over at the prosecutor, Eric Rosen. "Now, there is a plea agreement here. The Government's recommendation is within a guideline range sentence?"

"The Government's recommendation is below the guideline range, Your Honor," Rosen said.

Rob had explained to me earlier that sentencing guidelines were based on a point system calculated by the seriousness of the charges and the offender's record. In the case of fraud, the guidelines were generally calculated on the amount of money the victim had lost.

"I'm sorry?" the judge said, cocking her head.

"It's significantly below the guideline range, Your Honor."

"Below the guideline range?"

"Yes. I have the range calculated—the Court has a calculation of thirty-three to forty-one months, and the Government recommends in the plea agreement eighteen months."

The judge smiled. "Now, why can't all plea agreements be like this?"

"Good lawyering, Your Honor," Rob said. There were a few chuckles behind us.

"Mr. Vandemoer, this one count of this Information charging you with racketeering conspiracy, sir, how do you plead, guilty or not guilty?"

I tried to swallow.

"I plead guilty."

The judge asked the prosecutors to outline the evidence they would present if we were to go to trial.

Eric Rosen stood up and begin speaking. "The defendant was employed as a sailing coach at Stanford. As part of that job, he had a fiduciary duty to his employer. Instead, defendant accepted bribes from Rick Singer."

I looked down. This was going to be bad.

"In exchange for the bribes paid from Singer's charity, the defendant agreed to recruit Singer's clients to the Stanford sailing team—competitively, thereby providing them with the material benefit as a Stanford applicant. Effectively, defendant *sold* his recruiting spots allowed to him by Stanford," Rosen said, modulating his voice to add drama.

"In late December 2016 Singer brought an applicant to John Vandemoer. As part of the athlete recruiting process, Singer created a falsified sailing athletic profile to make it appear that this applicant was a real sailor. Although defendant did not help this candidate's application in any material way, this candidate was ultimately accepted to Stanford partly due to the fact that she had fabricated sailing credentials."

Molly Zhao. Why was he even talking about her?

"After her admission, Singer provided Vandemoer with $500,000 from the KWF charity, which was sent to the Stanford Sailing Program to be designated at the discretion of the coach to use an expendable amount. After making this payment, Singer brought Vandemoer another candidate, asking if it was possible to support him like he did the previous candidate, referring to the one I just mentioned. Vandemoer agreed to do this, exchanging a recruiting spot for money directed to"—Rosen paused—"the Vandemoer sailing program."

The Vandemoer sailing program. Jesus. I made a small pained noise and shifted in my chair. Rob glanced at me. He had warned me this was what would happen, that the prosecution would lay it on thick. He said I had to accept it. But I didn't. I didn't accept any of it.

"As partial payment for the recruiting spot, Singer sent Vandemoer $110,000 from the charity, made payable, again, to Stanford Sailing, care of the defendant. Although Vandemoer then proceeded to recruit the client, the candidate ultimately chose to attend Brown instead of Stanford. Singer then presented Vandemoer with a third candidate in early August of 2018, a high school student from Las Vegas who had minimal, if any, sailing experience. Nonetheless, Vandemoer agreed, almost immediately, to recruit this candidate in exchange for money, later determined on intercepted and recorded telephone calls, to be $500,000 as directed to a Stanford sailing account under his control.

"This candidate again ultimately chose to attend a different school, but on October 5, 2018, Singer and Vandemoer spoke on the phone, with Singer being in Boston. In the telephone call, Singer and Vandemoer agreed that the deal that he had arrived at was $500,000 per student, that a $160,000 payment that Singer was planning to make would be a deposit for the next student, and that Singer still owed Vandemoer $340,000 for that student. On October 25, 2018, Singer, from Boston, mailed Vandemoer a check for $160,000 from the KWF charity, as made payable to Stanford Sailing, care of the defendant."

I was seething. The things Rosen was saying were not true. Stanford received 100 percent of the Singer money. Admissions read zero applications. Not one of those kids got my support beyond sending them the pink envelopes offered by admissions based on their high school grades and test scores. I watched the court reporter transcribing Rosen's every word, and I knew his statements would be recorded forever and that there was nothing I could do to change that. I didn't understand how Rosen could take what Rick Singer, an admitted scam artist, had said and spew it to the judge.

"Who was the payee of all these checks?" Judge Zobel asked.

"They were paid from the charity," Rosen said.

"I understand. But *to whom?*" the judge asked pointedly.

"To the Stanford Sailing Program, care of the defendant."

"And the defendant took all the money?"

"He took the money into his sailing program," Rosen said. "There's not the allegations in this one that he took the money personally into his bank account."

"So he got no financial benefit personally?"

"The benefit was that he was able to purchase boats and things for his program. We do believe that there was a personal benefit, just not financially to his own bank account."

"But it's different from the other cases?" she asked.

Rob leaned over to me. "This is good for us."

"It's slightly different from the other—from all the other coaches and the other—which is why we've offered, I believe, a sentencing range that's about half of what the guidelines called for."

"Okay. Mr. Vandemoer." The judge peered down at me. "Can you please tell me in your own words what, if anything, you had to do with these three—or any program concerning students who not otherwise would be admissible or admitted into Stanford?"

This was what I had prepared for. I had to get it right.

"Yes, Your Honor. These—Rick Singer brought each of these— just like the prosecution said, brought each of these recruits to me.

The first one I ultimately, as the prosecution said, did nothing with. The other two, I inquired with admissions about their academic ability to be admitted into Stanford, and they gave me a pink envelope for each of those. In return, Mr. Singer said that those families would be interested in donating to the Stanford Sailing Program, to Stanford University if they were admitted."

"Did you know that you were doing something that violated the law?"

"I am clear now that I did, yes."

"At the time?"

I felt all eyes on me: the judge's, my father's, the prosecutors', the reporters'. Rob had told me this question about intent would be asked and that for me to get the plea deal, the prosecution needed me to say I had *intended* to break the law. I understood now that I had unwittingly been part of something that was illegal, but I absolutely had not intended to break the law. I didn't want to say that I had known it at the time because that wasn't true. Wasn't this lying under oath?

I let seconds tick by and then said, "At the time, yes."

There, I had done it.

"I find that the defendant understands the nature of the charges and the maximum penalty. I further find that the plea is voluntary and that there's a factual basis for it and accept it to Count 1 of this one-count Information. Lisa, what about sentencing?"

"So what about, maybe June 12 at 2:00?" the clerk said.

"That's fine with the Government," Rosen said.

The judge rose and we all stood up as she left the room.

"Good job," Rob said. "I know it hurts, but it will get better."

He and Scott gathered their things. I looked at my feet. I knew I would lose it if I met my father's eyes.

I was so sorry and sad that this mess had been dropped on my family: my mother, the elementary school teacher; my father, the renowned doctor; my wife, the Olympian; my kids. Oh god, I couldn't even think about my kids. One Google search and they would be the object of ridicule for the rest of their lives. My family would never escape this. I would never escape this.

Rob walked over to talk to Eric Rosen and the other prosecutors. Scott started up the aisle, and my father and I followed. I kept my eyes on the floor.

When Rob caught up with us, he said he'd let the press know he would be making a statement in front of the courthouse. "That will distract them. I'll walk out first. You go right to your car. Keep your eyes forward. Some of them will follow you. Just keep walking."

We all stepped into the elevator. Three reporters piled in with us. Scott looked at me and put his finger to his lips. We went down in awkward silence. Outside, reporters and camera operators jammed the sidewalk. Rob walked straight to a microphone stand. My father and I veered to the left, and a dozen or more reporters came with us, surrounding us as we hurried away.

We were moving fast, but the reporters, walking backward and shoving cameras in our faces, were keeping up.

"What did you do wrong if you didn't take any money?" one shouted.

"How did you meet Rick Singer?" another yelled.

"What do you want to say?"

"What do you want to say, Mr. Vandemoer?"

Finally, my father and I reached the doors of the parking garage and escaped the throng. My dad was breathing hard. "Wow," he said, shaking his head as he unlocked the car doors.

I couldn't look at him. We exited the garage and drove past the courthouse. Rob was still out there at the microphones, surrounded by reporters. My father's phone, which was sitting on the center console, buzzed. I could see the ID said "unknown caller."

"Don't pick it up," I said, just as he pushed the button and said hello.

"Mr. Vandemoer? I'm a reporter with the *New York Times*—"

"Dad, hang up!"

My phone went off. Unknown Caller. Then his phone rang again. Then mine.

In silence, we headed south out of the city.

Finally, my dad spoke. "Maybe see this as an opportunity to try something new, you know? Maybe you can go back to school."

"Uh-huh."

"Or you work your way gradually back into coaching."

"I don't know."

"Look at the Duke coach."

I grunted.

Eventually, my father went the safe route and started talking about the Red Sox.

"Think they can repeat?"

"Yeah," I said. "I don't know. Not without Sale."

"Yeah. The shoulder."

"Think Pedroia will be back?"

"Doubtful."

I finally got up the courage to look at my phone. I had 135 voice-mails. I started listening to some. Most were from friends offering support. But there were also some from people screaming, "Fuck you!" and "You greedy pile of shit." I was so freaked out, I deleted those right away. One man had called me twice, first claiming he had given me $75,000 in cash to get his kid into Stanford and that he needed it back or else I was "going to have a problem." In the next call, he said, "I hope you fucking die."

I had dozens of texts, too. Some were from people I knew well, wanting me to know they "still considered me a friend." I knew they meant that to be nice, but it stung. Patrick Dunkley, who had fired me that morning, had written to say he was praying for my family and me.

When we got home, I gave my mother a brief rundown about what had gone on and then went upstairs, kicked off my shoes, and called Molly. I was relieved to hear she hadn't gotten any calls from reporters and that she and the kids were fine. She said several team members had come by and brought her flowers and left cards for me.

"God, that's so nice," I said, feeling tears well up.

"I heard Bernard called a big coaches meeting," Molly said. "And he and Patrick were like, John did all of this bad stuff, and all the other coaches said, 'There's no way. That doesn't make any sense.' It took them a while to persuade them you had actually pled guilty. Now it's all over the news here."

"I can't believe this."

"You should shut down Instagram and everything," she said.

I agreed with her. But first, I wanted to look. When I hung up the phone, I opened Facebook and saw that a girl I had grown up with had posted about me. "I knew this all along. He's an awful person."

I also had several bizarre direct messages from a woman who said she was the head of a master's program at the University of Oregon.

"You're a money whore. You're disgusting. You're a disgrace."

I went to my email inbox. There were dozens of new messages. Half were media requests; the others were tirades against me. A member of the Stanford Board of Directors, whom I had met once, wrote, "How could you do this to Stanford?"

At around 8:30 p.m., I'd also received an email addressed to the "Stanford Community" from Stanford's president and provost. The subject line read, "The sailing case, and our resolve." It blew my mind that I had been included on that mailing list.

> By now many of you have seen the news that Stanford's head sailing coach was charged today, along with many others around the country, in an alleged scheme that involved payments intended to influence the admission of students to a number of U.S. colleges and universities.

> To the two of us, this is nothing short of appalling.

> Let us be clear: The conduct reported in this case is absolutely contrary to Stanford's values, and to the norms this university has lived by for decades. Today's news is a shock exactly because it so clearly violates our institutional expectations for ethical conduct.

> The charges brought by the Justice Department pertain to our former head sailing coach. But clearly, the case will prompt questions about our processes more broadly. We want to share some information about those processes.

> First and most importantly, every student admitted to Stanford must meet the university's high academic standards. Our admissions office conducts a holistic review of each

applicant, focused on academic excellence, intellectual vitality, extracurricular activity and personal context.

For students who have special talents—artistic, athletic, musical or otherwise—those talents are factored into the process. In the case of athletics, we have a process through which coaches can identify the most promising athletic recruits, for the consideration of the admission office. But such talents, athletic or otherwise, by themselves never ensure admission to Stanford.

Our resolve in these matters is as firm as ever. The integrity of our processes, and the ethical conduct of our people, is of paramount importance to Stanford.

The Justice Department investigation provided no evidence or indication that the conduct involved anyone at Stanford beyond the head sailing coach, including anyone associated with any other Stanford team. However, we are undertaking an internal process to confirm this is the case, across all of Stanford Athletics.

In addition, we will ensure that Stanford will not benefit from the monies that were contributed to the Stanford sailing program as part of this fraudulent activity. We are working to determine the most appropriate way to redirect the funds to an entity unaffiliated with Stanford, consistent with the regulations governing such gifts and in cooperation with the government.

We take these issues deeply seriously, and we will continue pursuing them mindful of our obligations as stewards of this institution, on behalf of everyone associated with Stanford.

I was shattered. The president and provost of Stanford University had written a letter about me? *This* was how they would learn my name after eleven years? What was going to happen to the team? If they were willing to cut me loose, what would stop them from just ending the sailing program? I thought there was a strong possibility Bernard would push for that. He'd want that clean break.

When I woke up, I was still wearing my clothes.

I went downstairs. My parents were sitting at the kitchen table drinking coffee. The *Cape Cod Times*, *The Boston Globe*, and the *New York Times*, still folded, were on the counter. To my horror, I saw that my picture was on the cover of the local paper and that the story was front-page news in the *Globe* and the *Times*. I picked up the *Globe*, scanned the article, and turned to the jump a few pages in. There was a large photograph of me walking into the courthouse—tight-lipped, distressed, shell-shocked. It was awful. Below my picture, there were smaller images of Felicity Huffman and Lori Loughlin. Huffman had been charged with paying Singer $15,000 to arrange for an accomplice to proctor her daughter's SAT exam and correct her answers afterward. Loughlin, with her husband, Mossimo Giannulli, had allegedly agreed to pay $500,000 to get their two daughters designated as recruits to the University of Southern California's crew team, even though neither of them rowed. The large-font headline read, "Rich and Powerful Are Arrested in College Bribery Scam."

"Not how I wanted to be in the newspapers," I said.

"I know," my mother said quietly.

My parents had offered to drive me to Logan Airport. About an hour into the trip, I got a call from John Morgan, the president of the Club 420 Association.

"I'm so sorry, John. I really tried," he said. "But we're going to need you to resign. There is too much publicity. We're getting a lot of pressure. Are you willing to resign?"

I said yes, sure, I understood. I told him I'd send him the resignation letter in the next few days. So now I had lost both of my jobs. We entered the dark mouth of the Ted Williams Tunnel and my heart rate spiked. What if a pack of reporters was waiting outside the airport? What if people recognized me in the terminal?

I was relieved to see that no one was waiting in ambush. Still, I felt like a spotlight was following me as I walked through the airport corridors wearing my Stanford backpack and pulling my Stanford carry-on. When I arrived at my gate and looked up at a mounted TV, I saw myself walking out of the courthouse. People all around me were reading *The Boston Globe*. This was unreal. I waited until the last minute to board and then kept my head down as I walked to my seat. On the flight home, I realized that I had no work to do for the first time in years. I watched movies all the way to San Francisco.

Molly was there to pick me up. We hugged each other for a long time.

As we approached Stanford, my dread grew. I didn't want any of our neighbors, my fellow coaches, to see me. Molly pulled into our driveway and I hurried into the house. I wanted to curl up into a ball. I didn't want daylight to come.

18

ake a few days," Molly said as she hoisted Nora's diaper bag over her shoulder. "Just do nothing."

I watched her walk out the door with both kids and then retreated to the couch. I had no intention of doing anything *but* nothing. I felt immobilized, sick with pity for myself, sick with grief about the dark cloud I'd dragged over the sailing team and, yes, over Stanford itself. Sacred Stanford.

I spent the next few days alternating between watching mindless TV and gorging myself on what the press was saying about the "college admissions scandal" and Operation Varsity Blues. Molly pleaded with me to stop reading about the case. But instead of doing that, without telling her, I put a Google alert on myself so that I wouldn't miss a single mention. I was shocked by how much attention the case was getting and how often my photograph appeared in the stories. I started to understand that because I'd been at the courthouse with Singer, I'd been an easy get for photographers. Now that those pictures of me had been syndicated, I seemed to have become, along with Singer, Lori Loughlin, and Felicity Huffman, a poster child for the scandal.

I was also astounded by how many of the stories twisted the facts or ignored them completely.

Scuttlebutt Sailing, an online publication Molly and I regularly read, as did much of the sailing community, snarked that I'd already been sentenced: "Getting the best sailors isn't easy either, regardless of how prestigious the degree. And after 11 years of trying, court documents state how Vandemoer had negotiated $770,000 in exchange for entrance to Stanford. The university claims to have been blindsided, Vandemoer claims the money was all for the program and not for him, and this pursuit of excellence has tattered his reputation and earned him a prison sentence of 18 months."

The *San Francisco Chronicle* ran a snippet of a wiretapped conversation between Singer and John B. Wilson, a CEO of a private equity and real estate development firm, who also happened to have a home on Hyannis Harbor. In it, Singer claimed to have approached me about Wilson's daughter. "I can send [Vandemoer] your $500,000 that you wired into my account to secure the spot for one of your girls," Singer told Wilson, according to court documents. "I asked him for a second spot in sailing and he said he can't do that because he has to actually recruit some real sailors so that Stanford doesn't catch on."

Singer was lying to him. He'd never spoken to me about John Wilson or his daughter. Yet any reader of the *Chronicle* that day would have reasonably assumed I had indeed said those things.

The *Palo Alto Daily Post* printed that I "wrote a fraudulent athletic profile for [Molly Zhao] when she was applying in early 2017." Not true. But how would my neighbors and fellow Palo Altans know that?

And then there were the snide columnists, like Eric Zorn of the *Chicago Tribune.* The paper's op-ed page ran a large photo of me leaving the courthouse with the headline "Admissions Scandal Highlights the Absurdity of Most Team Sports in Higher Education."

"Ahoy! Stanford has a varsity sailing team? Why?" Zorn's column began. "Why does the school offer special preference in admissions to those who know how to sail? Why does it pay a coach and assistant coach to oversee their training and send the team around the country to compete?"

A helpful link sent readers to the Stanford sailing team schedule to see for themselves just how outrageous our travel plans were.

I didn't just read the articles. I also wallowed in the nasty comments below them.

"Pigs at the trough."

"I talked to Vandemoer a few years ago about two of my junior sailing kids that were very interested in a Stanford education and joining the sailing team. He told me that academics and grade point averages were the prime requirement and athletic ability was a distant second. Boy, do I feel stupid."

"What an idiot. He gets paid SO well plus health and zillions of other perks from Stanford and lost all his past and future for a year's salary?"

"What happened to values? Isn't a part of coaching teaching the team sportsmanship and values? . . . disgusting."

I think a part of me wanted the daily flogging. It was hard not to feel that I *was* an idiot. I *was* disgusting.

When I wasn't staring at a screen, I studied the ceiling and brooded about how my family would survive without my paychecks, how we'd pay for health insurance, and where we were going to live when we lost our housing, which Stanford had notified me would happen on April 22. In occasional bursts of guilt-fueled energy, I raced around the house doing laundry, picking up the kids' room, unloading the dishwasher, and making preparations for dinner, then collapsed again, often in tears.

I'd been scheduled to put on sailing clinics all over the country, but one by one, they were canceled. Most hosts called me to let me know, but I found out the Annapolis Yacht Club had axed me when a friend sent a clipping from the *Capital Gazette*. The first line destroyed me: "Prior to March 12, John Vandemoer was one of the most respected figures in intercollegiate sailing."

I was required that first week to go to San Jose to check in with a pretrial probation officer and hand over my passport. I picked a day, forced myself to shower and get dressed, and then went quickly to the car, praying no one I knew would see me as I drove across campus. Once I'd made it to Highway 101, I relaxed a little and turned on the car radio. The newscast led with a story about Stanford firing me.

After I'd done what I needed to do, I stood outside the San Jose Federal Building and checked my phone. Adam Werblow had left a message.

"You okay?" Adam asked when I called back.

"Yeah. I don't know," I said, crossing the street to a sidewalk that skirted light rail tracks heading toward the downtown area. "I'm in San Jose. Just met with probation."

"Geez."

Adam said he'd heard from many fellow coaches who wanted to know what was going on with me and how they could help. The longtime waterfront director at St. Mary's had suggested starting a GoFundMe page for me.

"That's really nice," I said. "But no. I don't want that."

"A lot of the guys I talked to—I mean, it could have happened to any of us."

"I had no idea. He was a big donor, you know?" I said. "I was treating him like that. I didn't pay that much attention when he called."

"I've had those calls. We all have. They call at the worst time, but you feel like you have to talk to them. They're going on and on, and you're like, *right, yeah*. You're not listening at all. I get it."

I felt better after I talked to Adam. I walked a little more and then stopped at a coffee shop. As I waited, I glanced down at a newspaper on a rack and saw my picture on the front page. I reached down and quickly flipped the paper over. When the barista called my name, I grabbed my coffee and hurried to the exit.

Early the next week, Molly gently suggested I try taking the kids to or picking them up from daycare. I knew I had to do it. She had been killing herself handling everything—the kids, the grocery shopping, her job, to say nothing of the extreme stress of having to field questions about me from family and colleagues and close friends, a few of whom had asked whether she planned to divorce me. Even though I was terrified to walk by my fellow coaches' homes and to run into Stanford staffers who took their kids to the same daycare, I told Molly I'd do pickup that day.

When it was time to get the kids, I maneuvered the double stroller out the gate and started hoofing it down the sidewalk, keeping my eyes straight ahead. Maybe I'd get through this without having to talk to anyone.

"John!"

I looked over. Chris Miltenberg, the track and field coach, was playing baseball in his yard with his kids. His office had been next to mine in the athletics department. I used to see him every day.

He tossed the ball to one of his sons and trotted over. "How're you doing?"

"I'm okay."

"I'm so sorry about all this. It's awful. I can't believe the school did this to you."

"Thanks."

"Really, if you need anything, let me know."

Chris's few words boosted my confidence enough to propel me down the street. Maybe everyone didn't despise me. I steeled myself to walk into the daycare center. The teachers offered me fixed smiles—I knew they knew—as I collected the kids and got out fast. Then I aimed the stroller for the security of my front gate. Just as I was arriving, I noticed Tara and Steve Danielson, the Stanford field hockey coaches, coming across the street from their house.

Steve called out to me. "We saw you go by. We just wanted to tell you we're sorry about everything. We feel so bad for you. Stanford just sucks."

"Thank you. I appreciate it."

"Would you tell us what went on sometime when you feel like it?" Tara asked. "We'd like to hear the story because we don't want this to happen to us."

Over the next weeks, I heard that from other colleagues across the country. *Tell us what happened. We're scared of doing the same thing.* Some even thanked me for going through it all because it had prompted them to take a step back and think about how they handled big donors.

At Molly's urging, I agreed to talk to a therapist, something I'd never done before. I got an appointment with a doctor at Pacific Anxiety Group in Menlo Park. The name alone made me cringe. I was prepared to hate every minute of it, but I liked Dr. Tamara Hartl right away. She wasn't a blank wall, impassively asking how I felt. She seemed sympathetic. She even teared up as I told her my story.

Plus, she offered concrete advice. We went through exercises so I'd be better able to handle encounters in public. She helped me understand that if I waved to acquaintances and they didn't wave back, it didn't necessarily mean they had turned against me. They could be having a bad day and didn't feel like talking, or maybe they simply hadn't seen me wave.

I tried to remember that when I started venturing with great trepidation to the grocery store and the bank and the coffee shop. When I did see people I knew, they were almost all uniformly pleasant and wished me well. There was one glaring exception, though: my neighbor, Adam Cohen, whom I saw pass my house nearly every morning as he and his wife walked to get coffee. She always said hello. Adam always looked away. I had a million questions for him about Rick Singer, but I resisted the urge to confront him. I told myself nothing good could come of it.

Plus, we had more pressing worries. We were terrified Molly would lose her job because of me. If she did manage to hang on, we wondered whether there was any way she could persuade the PYSF board to cover our health insurance.

"Maybe it would help if you offered to explain everything to Stephanie," Molly said.

Stephanie Ashworth, the president of the PYSF Board of Directors, said she'd be happy to talk to me and invited the whole family out to her home in Woodside. Molly stayed behind with Stephanie's husband, Scott, and our kids while Stephanie and I went for a walk.

"I actually know some of the parents involved," she said as we headed down her tree-shaded street, passing large homes behind iron gates and tall hedges.

I wasn't shocked to hear that. I'd read that several of the parents charged lived in the area.

"It's disgusting what they did," she said.

"I agree. It's awful."

"But doesn't this stuff happen all the time?"

"You mean with donations?"

"People donate money, put their names on buildings or whatever, and their kids get in, right?"

"There are lots of buildings at Stanford with names on them, for sure," I said.

As we walked, I told her my story, about how Singer had wormed his way into my life and presented prospects who fit the exact profiles of students I'd told him I was hoping to find.

"Are you serious?" she asked.

I told her about the taped phone calls and the things Singer said that seemed meant to entrap me.

"This is incredible. It's like out of a movie."

And we talked about my bosses at Stanford, how they'd cheered Singer's hefty donations and then turned on me the minute the charges came out.

"The hypocrisy here," Stephanie said, shaking her head. "They're throwing you under the bus when clearly their admissions policies favor the children of donors."

We walked for more than an hour. When we were back in front of her house, she said, "Listen, if you're comfortable with it, I'd like to host a gathering for you and Molly with the board. Just tell them what you told me. Confidentially, of course."

"I'd like to do that," I said.

"Would it be okay if I told my father, too?"

I knew of Bruce Munro from the sailing world. He was a commodore at the St. Francis Yacht Club and a founding member of the National Sailing Hall of Fame. He had also been a prominent attorney in the city. I said yes.

ON THE WAY OVER TO THE Ashworth's house for the meeting the next week, Molly and I had the car radio on. An interview came on with Jamie Dimon, the chairman and CEO of JPMorgan Chase. His firm had just announced a five-year, $350 million program to train workers—including ex-convicts—for jobs.

"A lot of those people probably never should've been felons, or they've paid their price," we heard Dimon say. "They've got families. They've got kids. They can't get credit. They can't get a home. They struggle to get a job. And they deserve a second chance.

"These are not necessarily violent, lifelong criminals. These are people who made a mistake when they were young. I tell my friends, you made a lot of mistakes when you were young too; you just didn't get caught."

I looked over at Molly.

"Whoa," she said.

"Amazing."

Maybe Rob Fisher was right. The finance world might be a place I could find a job down the road.

Stephanie had asked us to come over early to spend time with her father before the board arrived. She'd filled him in on what had happened to me. After we talked for a few minutes, Bruce said, "Are you sure your lawyers did the right thing by having you plead guilty? I just don't see how this is racketeering. That's not at all how the law was intended to be used."

"I know. It's tricky," I said. "My lawyer said a lot of people, even some lawyers, would hear what happened with me and say how is that against the law? But he has a lot of experience with racketeering."

"But do you think maybe you should fight it?" Stephanie asked. "We don't think you got a great deal."

Molly glanced my way. I'd spent half the day close to tears. I knew Stephanie and her father meant well, but I couldn't think about fighting anything at that moment. Plus, we didn't have an extra couple of million dollars lying around.

"I trust his advice," I said.

The PYSF board included tech CEOs, attorneys, and executives at The Gap, Google, and other Bay Area companies who were united by their love of sailing. When everyone had arrived, we crowded around the Ashworth's dining table, and I told my story yet again. There was some head-shaking and a few "oh my gods" as I talked. My fears eased as I saw that they were sympathetic—even the Stanford alums.

"Can we give you references?" "What can we do?" "Can we get you to do some private coaching at PYSF?" they asked. We talked about our need for health insurance.

"We're going to make that happen," Stephanie said. Several of the board members nodded in agreement.

I was overwhelmed. We'd come in hoping to salvage Molly's job, and now they were offering to help me and my family.

The board's support gave me the confidence to pursue a few job leads. Even though I was in limbo and could very well be going to jail, Rob and Scott assured me the government wanted me to be employed. I was not a convicted felon until sentencing. Technically, I was fully eligible to work.

I was excited to learn that the San Francisco Yacht Club was looking for a new youth sailing director. I put in an application even though I was worried they might not want anything to do with me. The head of the waterfront, whom I knew, called me a few days later and confirmed my suspicions.

"We'd love to have you, and you are way overqualified," he said. "But I ran your name by some of the board members, and they were like, 'No way. He's too toxic.' I'm really sorry."

I also applied to write online sales descriptions for West Marine, the boat supplies retail chain I'd patronized for years. They rejected me. I volunteered to teach sailing to wounded veterans at the Warrior Sailing program. They said they didn't need an instructor but that I was welcome to donate.

I got the message. No one wanted any part of me.

In my downtime, and I had plenty of it, I obsessed over Stanford Sailing. I studied the real-time results, visualized the venues, imagined how each race was playing out. And while I craved information about the team, I also lived in constant fear of running into them. Molly had gotten the okay from her board to hire me to do some occasional private coaching sessions for PYSF, but that meant being on the same waters where Stanford sailed. I often checked with Clinton to find out what time his practice was so I'd be sure we wouldn't cross paths. Even then, I kept an eye out for those familiar white sails with red numbers tacking up Redwood Creek.

The court limited my ability to travel, but I was allowed to go to Massachusetts. Molly was running a large clinic in Southern California in early April, so I decided to take the kids to see my parents and my sister, Ann, who was also coming for a brief visit. On the flight from San Francisco to Boston, I happened to hit United Airline's million-mile frequent flyer status. The captain came back to congratulate me; the flight attendants offered me free drinks. My kids thought I was a superstar. When we landed, there was another announcement: "Welcoming John Vandemoer to the Million Miler club." As I made my way with Nicholas and Nora from the economy seats toward the exit door, I heard someone in First Class say, "Did he say John Vandemoer?" I wanted to disappear.

The week was chilly and damp, typical for early spring on Cape Cod, but it was a great relief to be there, out of the fray. When the kids were napping, I took long walks around the lake or sat on our dock, listening to a distant foghorn and lobbing small rocks into the water. I watched puffs coming across the dark surface and instinctively imagined how I would trim a sail to chase them. And I gazed at the old oak tree—my tree—which had been so battered by storms that only the trunk remained.

I'd made a plan to go to the Nixon Peabody offices in Boston that Thursday, partly to check in with Rob and partly to meet with producers from CBS's *60 Minutes*. Since my hearing, Rob had fielded dozens of interview requests on my behalf from *The Today Show*, *Good Morning America*, FOX News, MSNBC, CNN, and many others. He'd advised me to reject them all. They might sound sympathetic and say they wanted to give me a chance to tell my story, he said, but what they really wanted was to get me in front of their camera to grab a sound bite.

"If the spot is brutal, they'll play it repeatedly. If it puts you in a good light, it will get minimal airtime because it will be boring," he said.

The *60 Minutes* request, though, was something we both thought worth considering. We knew that even if the piece wasn't entirely about me, my portion of it would almost certainly be longer than a snippet. My kids weren't old enough to search my name on the internet yet, but they would be soon, and when they did, I wanted them to find something that was in my own words, that they might be able to point to with pride and say, "That's my dad." I also thought being able to explain myself on national television might help me in my job hunt.

A CBS producer had told me that if I wanted to do a preliminary interview, they would come to Boston whenever I was in town. Rob had arranged for them to meet me at Nixon Peabody. Not surprisingly, they asked excellent, probing questions, and I felt cheered by the fact that they seemed most interested in hearing that Bernard Muir said he knew Rick Singer.

After they left, Rob and I spoke for a while in his office. When I was getting ready to go, he said, "You know, John, I think about this a lot. I wonder, should we have fought this?"

I braced myself for what he was going to say.

"And then I stack everything up, and I think, no, we did the right thing."

I exhaled. I had to believe I'd made the right decision. And it was comforting to hear Rob say he'd been thinking about my case, that he hadn't just moved on to his next client. It made me feel like he cared.

19

Our friends Anne and Ian Wright offered to let my family live rent-free at least through the summer in a home they owned in Moss Beach, a small coastal community about twenty miles south of San Francisco. With the deepest gratitude, we took them up on it.

Before the move, I threw myself into cleaning out our Stanford house. I went at it like it was a crime scene, stripping it of any evidence that we had been there at all. There was no way I was not going to get our damage deposit back. I would at least leave with my head held high about that.

I gathered up eleven years of Nike gear embroidered or printed with "Stanford Sailing" and stuffed it into big black trash bags. Then I drove the bags to a Goodwill drop-off spot within view of the university's football stadium. It seemed a fitting place to dump it all.

On April 20, Molly and I loaded our cars to go "over the hill," as locals called the trip over the Santa Cruz Mountain ridge that divided the bustling South Bay from the much slower-paced Coast-side. Driving away from Stanford was gut-wrenching. My children were born here. I'd coached the most amazing kids here. I'd built my career here. And now we were leaving it forever.

THE WRIGHT'S SPANISH-STYLE STUCCO HOUSE WAS tucked in a hill-side neighborhood above Highway 1 and had a back deck with views over cypress trees to the Pacific. It couldn't have been nicer, but I was too busy carrying boxes and suitcases and trying to keep track of the kids to pay much attention. I was also preoccupied with checking Stanford's regatta results. The team had two important events that weekend: the two-day interconference Admiral's Cup, hosted by the US Merchant Marine Academy in King's Point, New York, and the Pacific Conference Women's Championships at the US Sailing Center in Long Beach, California. I was constantly refreshing the ICSA real-time results page on my phone.

The women in Long Beach were crushing it. They cruised to Stanford's fifteenth straight conference championship in light winds and bright sun and qualified for the next month's nationals in Newport, Rhode Island. Back East at the Admiral's Cup, the coed squad contended with big wind, up to forty-two knots, off King's Point, where the East River meets the Long Island Sound. Stanford had struggled early but done better in later races. The team was in sixth place at the end of day one, forty-three points behind Dartmouth.

After Molly and I got the kids settled that first night, I lay in bed, wide-eyed and frazzled and feeling sorry for myself. I thought about the women's conference championship and the victory celebration I had missed. I'd written notes of congratulations to Clinton and one of the players. I'd wanted to text them all but stopped myself from doing it. What right did I have to inject myself into their happy day?

I also thought about the coed group in New York. I wondered how they were feeling after their tough day. This was a big interconference regatta; the results were often telling about how teams would fare at nationals. We'd have to do better off the starting line, for sure, if we wanted to move up tomorrow. I worried that we weren't ready.

They weren't ready. *They*, not *we*, I reminded myself. It wasn't my job to wonder about any of it—if they were prepared for nationals or if they would be strong off the start or how hard the wind would be blowing. I wasn't part of it anymore.

I lay there in the dark, telling myself to find good things to think about. Molly was sleeping next to me. We were in a beautiful place. We had kind, generous friends. We were healthy. We had two beautiful kids. A breeze was blowing through the open windows, and I could hear waves breaking on rocks a half-mile or so away. I followed their cadence with my breath and smelled the piney, moisture-laden salt air and found it familiar and comforting. It smelled like home. *We'll be okay*, I told myself. *I'll be okay*.

In the morning, though, the reality of what we had lost was all too clear. Nicholas woke up with his usual inquisitiveness in overdrive. He wanted to know why we weren't in the "blue house." When could he play with his friends? When could we go home? When could we go back to Stanford? Stanford this and Stanford that. I was surprised by the depth of feeling he seemed to have for the school, even at age three.

I realized then that I had an obligation not to ruin Stanford for my sweet son. It was ruined for Molly and me. I promised myself I wouldn't badmouth it in front of him. I felt like a jilted spouse biting my tongue about my cheating ex for the sake of the kids. Some days, though, it seemed impossible to hold it in.

I stewed over how to let Nicholas know that we were not going back to the blue house and that he was going to have to switch daycares. Even more agonizing was telling him something about what had happened to me—to us. One day when we were sitting together on the front steps, he asked why I didn't go to work anymore.

I spoke slowly and quietly. "Well, I was involved with a really bad guy, and I ended up doing bad things with that guy, not knowing I was doing bad things."

"Bad things?" he said, squinting up at me.

"Yes, but I didn't mean to. I made a big mistake, and I have to pay the price for it. But because I made the big mistake, I'm going to grow and learn and be a better person."

"It was a big mistake?"

"Yeah, a pretty big one. But it will be okay."

Every morning after that, when Nicholas was leaving with Molly and Nora to go to daycare, he'd stop at the door, turn back to look at me, and say, "Don't make any mistakes today, Dad. Especially don't make any *big* mistakes."

It destroyed me.

NOT LONG AFTER WE MOVED, OUR friends Glenn and Nancy Reynolds, whose son Sam sailed with Molly's program and lived in nearby Half Moon Bay, invited us over for dinner. Glenn ran Water Solutions, a small company that designed potable water systems and specialized in challenging projects. I happened to know one of his employees, Becca Carlton. Becca had been the Stanford assistant rowing coach until 2016. Over dinner, I talked about my futile job hunt.

"We're always looking for people," Glenn said. "You don't happen to have a degree in geology kicking around, do you?"

"Actually, I do," I said with a laugh.

"Seriously?" he said.

"Yup, seriously. B.S. in geology."

"You should come work for me!"

I knew how little work in the sciences could pay, and I had a growing mountain of debt. My brother-in-law's generosity could go only so far. He'd covered Rob Fisher's retainer and other legal fees but had let me know he couldn't offer anymore. As grateful as I was that Glenn had suggested working for him, I didn't think it was the right direction for me. And besides, I might very well be going to jail in a few months.

IN THE MEANTIME, I ENROLLED IN a Cornell online class in project management. By then, Molly and I had broken into our 401K plan, but there were tax breaks if we spent some of the money on education. We told ourselves it was an investment in our future. I thought the coursework might eventually help me land a job at one of the tech giants in the area.

But that was way down the road. I needed to make more money now. The private coaching sessions I was doing at PYSF for Molly were not bringing in nearly enough to cover our bills. I was certified at the highest level in instructor training, and I'd even written some of the certification materials. I was also licensed to teach powerboat handling. I thought I might use those credentials to get paid to train coaches and instructors, but I could do that only if I was still in good standing with US Sailing. I had no idea what they thought of me.

I emailed Jack Gerhart, the group's executive director, to ask about my status and to offer to answer any questions he had. I explained briefly in my email how prohibitive the cost of fighting the legal case would have been and why I had decided to plead guilty. I asked him to please not lump me in with all the other coaches in the case. There was plenty of public evidence to prove that I hadn't kept the money for myself. He didn't have to take my word for it.

Jack said he'd see what he could do. A short time later, the US Sailing president wrote to say she felt for me and wished me well. She added that she'd heard from only one member who wanted the group to sanction me. That sounded promising. A few days later, though, I got a message from another administrator saying that the organization had decided they wanted me to self-suspend my credentials. When everything was over, they'd be happy to help me get them back.

Rob contacted US Sailing on my behalf to ask just what they meant by "when everything is over" and what I would have to do to get my credentials back. They never replied. I didn't know where I stood with the group until I went online to pay my membership renewal fee and saw that my log-in had been blocked.

IN LATE APRIL AND EARLY MAY, the Google alerts I had put on myself and the case became active again. The news broke that Molly Zhao's billionaire parents had paid Rick Singer a staggering $6.5 million after she had been admitted to Stanford. No wonder Singer had been so casual about donating $500,000 to the Stanford sailing program on the family's behalf.

According to the Zhao family attorney, Singer had told the parents that "the money would go toward scholarships, athletic teams, staff salaries, and programs that help students who otherwise could not afford to attend Stanford."

At about the same time, it also came out that another Chinese family had paid Singer $1.2 million to get their daughter, Sherry Guo, flagged as a soccer recruit by the Yale head coach, Rudy Meredith. Meredith admitted he had pocketed $400,000 from Singer to secure her spot. Molly Zhao had been expelled from Stanford and Sherry Guo had left Yale but the parents, all of whom were introduced to Singer by a financial consultant, were not charged.

Lawyers for both families said Singer exploited both the Chinese communities' general lack of knowledge about the US college admissions process and the lengths wealthy Chinese parents were willing to go to get their children into elite US universities. Test prep and private college counseling were part of a multibillion dollar industry in China that was tantalizingly ripe for swindlers and con artists like Rick Singer.

The week after the Zhao and Guo revelations, my phone pinged with more alerts. Felicity Huffman had pleaded guilty to paying Singer to boost her daughter's SAT scores. Laura Janke, a former assistant women's soccer coach at the University of Southern California, also admitted her guilt, acknowledging that Singer made direct payments to a private soccer club controlled by her and another defendant in exchange for creating fake athletic profiles, including ones for Lori Loughlin's daughters. News outlets worldwide picked the stories up, often adding round-ups of what had already transpired in the case. There I would be again, next to a rehashing of my crime. It was bad enough that I kept appearing in the media; even more upsetting was how often Stanford Sailing popped up in the coverage. The team didn't deserve any of this.

I decided to reach out to some sailing team alums, hoping I could explain myself over lunch or coffee and answer any questions they might have. If they didn't want to talk about the case, I added in my notes to them, that was fine, too. I would just like to see them again. I started easy, with people I already knew were supportive. Those meetings went well.

But one lunch, with a recent alum I'd recruited and thought the world of, brought me back to the reality of what havoc I had wrought. She was working at an architecture firm in the city and agreed to meet me during her break.

We made small talk for a while. Then she said she'd been in touch with some fellow team members.

"I have to tell you," she said. "We were advised to take Stanford Sailing off our résumés."

"What?" I felt like I'd been knifed. "Oh, god, I'm so sorry."

"I didn't, but—"

I sat in silence, twisting my napkin.

"I just don't understand how you could have done these things," she said.

"I thought I was taking regular donations and getting players who could help the team and also, you know, possibly donate."

She pressed her lips together and looked at me.

"At the time, it seemed like a good, you know . . ." I trailed off.

I heard how flimsy my explanation sounded. I'd repeated the story so many times, I'd started to confuse myself about what I had been thinking and when I had been thinking it.

"But didn't you know it was wrong, taking that money?"

"I see it now," I said. "But back then, no. I didn't."

"I don't get how you wouldn't."

"I made a mistake. I didn't pay attention. I didn't ask enough questions. It hurt you guys tremendously and I'm so sorry about that."

"Okay," she said coolly, taking her purse off the back of her chair and standing up. "Well, I have to go back to work."

I felt awful as I walked back to my car. I would never forgive myself for making former team members question whether they should keep Stanford Sailing on their résumés.

20

In mid-May, Rob forwarded me the presentencing report from probation, written by Martha Victoria. It would carry a lot of weight with the judge, he said, and would help determine an appropriate sentence. Our job was to read it right away and ask for corrections if we found things we disagreed with.

I was out on the water in one of PYSF's Boston Whalers after finishing a private coaching session when I opened the document on my phone. I let the engine idle and drifted toward the docks as I read the report. One thing jumped out at me immediately. Martha said that the third and final check from Rick Singer had been written directly to me. That wasn't true. None of the checks had been written to me. They were all to Stanford. I emailed Rob to point out the mistake.

He replied immediately. "That's strange. They aren't saying you took the money, but they are saying a check was written to you. Let me talk to probation."

Rob called me that evening. "So, I asked them to send me the check images. I'm forwarding them to you. That last check *is* written out to 'Stanford Sailing John Vandemoer.' You didn't see that?"

"What? No, I never opened that envelope. I saw it come in and recognized Singer's return address and just walked it down to the development office."

I thought back to that October phone call when Singer had asked me where I wanted his $110,000 donation to go. He'd suggested sending it directly to me, and I said he should send it to Stanford, just as he'd done before.

That was jarring, but the most significant finding in the presentencing report was that Stanford had suffered no financial loss. *No loss*. This, Rob told me, was huge. Sentencing guidelines in fraud cases are typically calculated on the basis of the amount of money the victim lost. If there was no loss, how could there be a victim? Having the judge accept this conclusion from probation would make a big difference in the sentencing guidelines that were used in my case. It would also likely set precedent for other defendants in the college admissions case who had signed similar plea agreements.

Rob also submitted a sentencing memorandum to the judge, as did the prosecution. The government's was a scathing twenty-five-page report written to justify the prison time they sought for me. Included were excerpts from the three October 2018 phone calls Singer had made to me. I wasn't surprised to see that the transcripts made it obvious that I hadn't been able to hear much of what Singer had been saying. The FBI had flagged many sections as "inaudible." But the government insisted these conversations were evidence of my guilt—and pointed to one exchange as being especially damning. My heart sank as I read it.

According to the transcript, Singer had said on October 24, "But what I wanted to—what I wanted to do was I just want to make sure that we're confirmed that, you know, going forward, I'm going to be able to at least potentially have a spot with you. It'll probably be an athlete like Molly, who wasn't an actual sailor. And then I'll . . . put together the profile for her, and put all the major regattas that I come up with, from the internet, and bring somebody to you. And then, again, we'll make a payment to you again."

Like Molly, who wasn't an actual sailor . . .

I was floored. I had no recollection of Singer saying Molly wasn't a sailor. How could I have not paid attention to that? I had been in such a hurry to get off the phone.

The prosecution's memo also refuted probation's conclusion that Stanford had suffered no loss. In addition, they were requesting a change in the charge, saying they had made an error in the original plea agreement.

It was complicated, but what I understood from Rob was that the prosecution wanted to switch the sentencing guideline analysis from fraud to bribery. This would allow them to base sentencing guidelines not on the amount of money lost, but on the amount that was discussed—even if it never changed hands. The new charge would also bump up the sentencing guideline range. My plea agreement stated the range was from thirty-three to forty-one months; the government was now saying it should be thirty-seven to forty-six months.

Rob told me that in asking for this change the prosecution had effectively broken the plea agreement I had signed. The wrong sentencing guidelines had been used. As a result, I could get out of the deal if I wanted to. I was shocked. I'd been told plea agreements were ironclad. And now I could retract it?

"They'll just come after you again," Rob said. "But the option is there."

Even more mystifying was what the government's sentencing memo said about what they were seeking for a prison term. Despite their push for a charge that carried higher sentencing guidelines, they were now asking for only thirteen months. My plea deal had been for eighteen months. I didn't know what to think.

Rob's memo focused on showing the court who I was as a father and coach; to that end, he included many excerpts of letters written in my defense by colleagues and friends. He also argued that probation would be an appropriate sentence for me.

ONE EVENING, AFTER THE KIDS HAD gone to bed relatively easily, Molly and I each got a beer and went out to sit on the deck. It was a gorgeous night, warm and breezy and fog-free, and there was still light in the sky on the western horizon. We sat in silence for a while, sipping our beers and enjoying the view.

"So I'm going to do some interviews next week," I finally said. "Rob set them up. With *The Wall Street Journal*, the *New York Times*, and *The Boston Globe*."

"Can you do that? Before you get sentenced?"

"They won't run them until after the hearing."

"Do you know what you're going to say?"

"I'm going to say that I take responsibility for what happened, you know, that I made a mistake. That I was misguided. And that I'm doing what's best for my family, that it doesn't matter that my career is over—"

"John," Molly said, putting her bottle down on the small table next to her chair. She leaned forward and looked me in the eyes. "You do not have to be a martyr for us."

She finished her beer, then stood up and said, "I'm getting another drink."

I stared after her. What did she mean by that? I'd assumed she would be proud of me for sacrificing myself for the good of the family.

"What do you want me to say?" I asked when she came back.

"Say you didn't do it! Say Stanford threw you under the bus! This is the first time you'll be able to say what happened. Say it!"

"I don't think I'm allowed to," I said. Rob had told me that when you plead guilty, you can't then walk it back in the press. The prosecution could use that against you if things fall apart. It was way too risky.

Molly shook her head slowly and looked away.

On June 9, I took a red-eye to Boston. Molly would follow me out on the eleventh. Our friend Anne Wright would stay with Nicholas and Nora in Moss Beach. I went straight to Nixon Peabody, and when Rob brought me into his office, he told me he'd just received Stanford's impact statement.

"It's the mildest one I've ever seen," he said, and began reading it to me.

"'Although Mr. Vandemoer's conduct resulted in donations to the Stanford sailing team, Stanford views those funds as tainted and is in discussions with the California Attorney General about an appropriate way for those funds to be used for public good. Stanford does not wish to benefit in any way from Mr. Vandemoer's conduct. Stanford also recognizes that Mr. Vandemoer took responsibility for his actions early in the criminal process and that he did not personally receive any payment from the scheme.'"

Rob looked up at me. "That's really good for us."

The first interview I had scheduled was over the phone with Kate Taylor, a reporter for the *New York Times*. Though Rob and his team had helped me come up with the points I wanted to make, I was so nervous that I stumbled over my words and forgot what I had planned to say. I was sure I'd botched it. The next day, I met with *The Boston Globe* and *The Wall Street Journal*. Those interviews felt better to me. After I was done, I walked to Macy's and bought two suits in a buy-one, get-one deal. I needed one for court, and I told myself I'd get use out of both of them when I started going out on job interviews.

Molly arrived later that evening.

"Can I do my statements for you?" I asked. I planned to make a statement to the judge and one to the press after the hearing. I'd been practicing them alone in front of a mirror.

"Sure." She was sitting on the hotel bed. I stood in front of her.

Before I was halfway through the first one, she held up one hand and said, "Stop."

"What?"

"What are you doing?"

"What do you mean?"

"You sound so *defeated*. Why aren't you standing up for yourself?"

"I am standing up for myself."

"No, you're not. You're like a beaten puppy."

"What does that mean?"

"This isn't you, John. Stand up straight! Put your shoulders back! Be proud of who you are and what you're saying. Let everyone see the person I know and love."

It meant everything to me that I had Molly's support after the hell I'd put her through. They could throw me in jail, but they couldn't take that from me.

IN THE MORNING, MOLLY, MY PARENTS, my sister Jennifer, and I gathered in Nixon Peabody's sunny corner conference room. It was a painfully beautiful late-spring day. Beyond the plate glass window, the harbor shimmered and dozens of boats were under sail. When it was time to go over to the courthouse for the 2 p.m. hearing, Scott came to get us and said we'd all drive over together in a Suburban.

When we stood up, my mother said, "John, wait."

I turned toward her.

"I have something for you." She pulled out an index card and handed it to me. A four-leaf clover was taped to one side of it. I recognized it as my mother's signature gift for significant events. I never knew how or when she found the clovers, but she always came up with them. Later, I'd read what she had written on the back of the card: "Dearest John, Keep this close to you. Remember how much I love you, always! You are my beloved son."

I smiled and slipped the card into my jacket pocket. "Thank you."

"Love you," she said.

We parked just around the corner from the courthouse entrance and piled out of the SUV, with Rob and Scott leading the way. Molly and I held hands as we followed them. The rest of my family trailed behind. The moment we rounded the corner, reporters were on top of us, shouting and pushing.

"Are you going to apologize?" one yelled. "Coach Vandemoer, any message for your former athletes? They looked up to you!" another shouted. A camera hit me in the head. The crowd pressed in and banged Molly up against the building. I tried to pull her in closer to me. I was worried about my mother getting jostled behind us. We finally reached the courtroom doors.

"That was nuts," Molly said as she rubbed her shoulder.

We all took an elevator to the fifth floor, and when we stepped out, reporters swarmed us again. Rob told them that I would be making a statement in front of the building after the hearing.

In Courtroom 12, we took our places. My lawyers went over to talk to the prosecutors and then to Martha Victoria, who was sitting in the jury box. I sat alone with both my knees jackhammering, looking around again in disbelief at the cop-show trappings of the courtroom. Rob and Scott came back, and Judge Zobel entered.

When she got to the bench, she asked all the lawyers and me to approach her.

"This was sent to me last night," she said, handing out a sheet of paper to each of us. I saw that it was a rant about what an awful person I was.

"This is a big deal to get this because no one has my email," Judge Zobel said. "I'll have the marshals investigate. But I want you to know this won't impact me at all in the proceeding. Are you okay with carrying on?"

We said we were.

Rob had warned me that the first part of the hearing was not going to be about me; it would be about the technicalities of sentencing guidelines.

"It's going to sound like we're doing our taxes," he said.

He was right. I tried to follow along, but the numbers and terms Rosen was tossing out were stupefying: "If you look at Paragraph 18 of what he pled guilty to and 18B, Title 18 United States Code Sections 1341 and 1346 relating to honest services mail fraud, and then Predicate Act D, Title 18 United States Code Section 1343 and 1346 relating to honest services mail fraud . . ."

Rosen grew animated when he turned to probation's finding that Stanford had suffered no loss.

"I just want to make sure the record is clear. The parties agree that there was a loss here between I believe $550,000 and $1.5 million," he said.

"What's the loss?" the judge asked.

"The loss here is Stanford suffered, you know, significant pecuniary loss, and I laid that out in our sentencing memo."

"No," the judge said. "I was looking at Stanford's own letter, and they say that although the defendant's conduct resulted in donations to the Stanford program, they think they are so tainted that they want to give it away. So what are the losses?"

"I'm talking about loss that Stanford suffered—the guidelines are very clear. You have actual loss, you have intended loss, and when the amount is difficult to calculate, use the gain gotten by the defendant. The parties had agreed that the—both the actual and the intended loss—"

"The gain to *whom?*" Judge Zobel asked.

"The gain to the defendant, which in this case—"

"What's the gain to the defendant?"

"$610,000 into his sailing program," Rosen said.

"It's not *his* gain," the judge said sharply. "He gave it to the university."

"It absolutely *is* his gain," Rosen said, matching her tone. "He benefited significantly by allowing it to boost his program, buying new boats. It was absolutely for his intended benefit. It didn't go directly into his pocket, but it certainly went to his benefit. The university acknowledges that by giving away the tainted funds. They don't want it—"

"Did they give away the boats, too?"

I heard some laughter behind me.

"I don't know what's happened with the boats, Your Honor."

Rosen and the judge continued to spar. Rob leaned over and touched my knee.

"I'm not going to say anything here," he said under his breath. "The prosecution is digging themselves into a hole. The judge is doing our work for us. We're just going to listen."

After another lengthy exchange, Judge Zobel seemed to have had it with Rosen.

"I accept the calculation by the probation officer with all of the details that she has given us. I do not find any loss by—that I can in any way calculate by Stanford or based on the letter that Stanford has sent and will not do any further—I will make no further attempt to try to figure out what loss there might be or what gain there might have been. So your objection to that ruling is noted. And we end up with the same calculation that I said previously, a total offense level of 18, Criminal History Category I, and the guideline range of twenty-seven to thirty-three months."

Wait, what? Where had that come from? She was talking about nearly three years in prison!

"And I will now hear the Government's recommendation," the judge said.

21

Eric Rosen asked whether he could get some water, and then launched in.

"Judge, on March 12th of 2019, fifty individuals were charged by complaint, indictment, and information. Defendant John Vandemoer, the former sailing coach at Stanford, was the first coach to plead guilty, the first to be sentenced, as we know. The sentence you impose today, Your Honor, will set the tone for these cases going forward.

"The Government strongly believes that a sentence of imprisonment here will send a powerful message to the defendant, to the other defendants in this case, and to those considering using bribery and fraud to secure college admissions at elite universities for children, students, and clients. The message is simple, but it does need to be said. If you pay or receive bribes, if you lie and cheat, and if you engage in a scheme that ultimately results in the theft of a college admissions spot from someone who deserves it, you will be criminally prosecuted, and you will go to prison . . .

"And why is the sentence of imprisonment needed here? It is needed because this case goes far beyond John Vandemoer and the $610,000 he agreed to accept. Rather, the damage that the college admissions scheme inflicted, as outlined in numerous indictments, complaints, and information, was significant and far-reaching."

Now I understood why Rosen was fighting so hard, even though he'd told Rob back in March that he wouldn't "pound the fist." He was thinking about the cases to come; precedent would be set. He couldn't afford to have the judge go lightly on me.

Rosen began reading letters from high school students that the *New York Times* had published in March after the admissions scandal had come to light. I heard "appalled," "horrible," "terrifying," "dishonorable," "unfair." Even though I knew I had not prevented any student from applying to or being accepted at Stanford, I felt crushed by the kids' outrage. It was horrible to be even the smallest part of this thing. He read more letters and I sank in my chair. I felt my face flush.

"I do not dispute the premise of the defendant's sentencing memorandum, which is that the defendant is a good person. I do not dispute that the defendant loves his family and his children, the defendant loved his employment at Stanford. . . . The defendant appears to be a great sailing coach.

"As Your Honor knows, good people sometimes do bad things, and the defendant's good work should be taken into account at sentencing."

Rosen pointed out that probation in my case would be "a slap on the wrist for the defendant" and requested "thirteen months of imprisonment, which is sufficient but not greater than necessary to achieve a just result."

Back to thirteen months. I hung my head while Rosen laid out the case for his requested sentence.

Then Rob stood up and began speaking without notes. "Your Honor . . . As I said multiple times today, as Your Honor noted at my client's change of plea months ago, he did not benefit from these bribes. They didn't go to him. They went to Stanford. This is a gentleman with his heart in the right place.

"What you have here is somebody who has been punished enormously, and jail is not going to do anything more than punish his own family. He has—when I first met him, he had a great job at Stanford. He was making good money. He lived in housing at Stanford. He has two young kids. He had a car stipend. He was living his dream. He gave everything to those students on that sailing team.

"Once this indictment dropped and he pled guilty a couple of months ago before you, he lost his job, he lost his housing. He and his kids had to move to another home that they're living in thanks to friends of the family. They lost their health insurance. They lost their car stipend. This man has been absolutely crushed. And given the media attention surrounding this case, and not just because of Mr. Vandemoer, because of the celebrities involved here, as Mr. Rosen said, fifty other individuals—and I would like to note of all those individuals, everybody *but* Mr. Vandemoer gained something. Even the parents who may have paid $15,000 so their son or daughter's ACT test could be changed, they gained something. He got nothing.

"He gave every single dime to his sailors, to Stanford, and they still have the money. He could have pocketed that. He didn't . . . and he has been absolutely crushed because of this. So let the media report today, let it be heard wide that if you do something like this in the future, you will lose everything."

I looked at my hands as Rob went on. "Your Honor . . . what you will have if you send Mr. Vandemoer to prison for thirteen months or six months or whatnot, he will end up, I'm pretty confident, serving more time than potentially some of the parents who paid a bribe to either Mr. Singer, that went to a school, or influenced the SAT or the ACT that colleges may have relied on. Their guidelines could be three to six [months], and I can assure you that many of them . . . the multimillionaires that are involved in this case did not lose their housing, did not lose their health insurance, are not worried about their car breaking down . . .

"He's a dad of two very young children . . . and those are the folks who are going to suffer if he goes to prison. . . . This gentleman has lived a wonderful life. He was a great son to his parents, a great college student, who's been an impeccable coach. Friends and family and ex-sailors love him."

Rob continued. "Sometimes there's no other way to punish people. They may be a danger to the community and need a specific deterrent to teach them a lesson. Even the Government agrees that's really not the case here. This is a unique situation with an individual who has learned his lesson and will do everything he can to get back to society and his family. And with that, we ask for a one-year term of probation."

"Mr. Vandemoer, do you wish to say anything?" Judge Zobel asked.

I said I did. This was what I had prepared for. I got to my feet. I thought of Molly behind me and drew my shoulders back.

"Your Honor, the last three months have given me a lot of time to reflect on my mistake and who I am. I have learned many things through this reflection and know two things to be true. I spent my life trying to be a good, moral person, but here I made a terrible mistake, and my mistake impacted the ones I care about the most in ways I could not imagine. I would like to take the time to apologize to the ones I have hurt. First the Government and the Court, I took up your precious time and resources. For that I am sorry.

"Next, Stanford, an amazing school with incredible people. The students, alumni, staff, and faculty do not deserve to be looked at under the cloud that I have brought over them. I am truly sorry for bringing you into this mess. You do not deserve it.

"To the current sailing team, to the coaching staff, to the team's alumni, and the collegiate sailing community, I am devastated that this has impacted you all. I'm devastated that the program and the sport would be looked at poorly because of my actions. You had no part in it and you did not deserve it. I have spent my career stressing that some things, namely integrity and your reputation, are more important than winning. In this manner I completely failed to live up to that standard. I want to thank you all for your support and forgiveness these last three months and will be eternally sorry to you all."

Then my voice snagged. I took a breath, trying to steady myself.

"Most importantly, to my family and friends. I'm sorry to have dragged you into this. My friends, I am sorry that you had to question who I am and how you will act around me, but I thank you for standing by me and seeing me for who I am and not only for my mistake. My sister Jennifer, who has been an amazing source of support that always reminds me of who I am. I love you and I'm truly sorry. My father, I dragged your good name into the scandal. That will haunt me forever. You have stood by me and reminded me to keep my head high. I love you and I am truly sorry. My mother, who will never let me forget my passion and fire to be a better person, to be a father, to be a husband. I love you, and I'm truly sorry. My wife, Molly, has shown unbelievable courage and bravery through all of this. You are a true role model for our children and for me. I love you, and I am truly sorry. My children, Nicholas and Nora, are too young to understand this yet, but it won't be long. Someday soon I'll have to explain to them that their dad is certainly not perfect and that he makes mistakes. I hope they will in time also see someone who takes responsibility for his mistakes and tries to handle it with grace and honor. I love you, and I'm truly sorry.

"In the last three months I've been fired, put my family's financial security in jeopardy, and caused us to lose our housing. My career that I have worked at passionately for twenty years is gone, and my freedom is in jeopardy, endangering my ability to be there for my kids. I deserve all of this. I caused it, and for that I am deeply ashamed.

"Finally, Your Honor, I want to tell you how I intend to live from this point forward. First, I will never again lose sight of my values and who I am as a friend, son, brother, husband, and father. Second, I will not curl up and feel sorry for myself. I made a mistake. I am accepting responsibility, and I am bound and determined to move forward with my life in a way that honors the love and support that I have gotten over the last three months from my family, my friends, and my sailors. Thank you for your time."

I sat down. I was trembling. I felt as if I'd just crossed a canyon on a high wire. Now we would hear from the judge. I held my breath.

"I have read the transcripts of telephone calls by Mr. Singer to Mr. Vandemoer," she said. "And although there's no question that Mr. Vandemoer participated in this, Mr. Singer *pushed*, he really pushed, and Mr. Vandemoer sort of responded by saying, yes, yes. That clearly was a mistake. I have no doubt that he knew what he was doing was probably wrong and he saw the benefit to his program. From what I know about the other cases, which is not very much, there appears to be a general agreement, certainly among probation officers who are handling collectively all of these cases, that Mr. Vandemoer is probably the least culpable of all of the defendants in this group of cases. I have not heard of anybody who is less culpable.

"Certainly the parents are in a different position. The other coaches benefited for themselves. They took money for themselves. He did not do that. All the money that he got went directly to the sailing program . . . So the fact that he, as best as I understand, was the least culpable of all of the coaches certainly has something to say about what the sentence should be."

I felt a spark of hope.

"I have read the letters of support, all twenty-seven of them, and I must say, they are an extraordinary group of letters. The usual letters are perfunctory, one paragraph long, and that's it. These are thoughtful letters, every last one of them, thoughtful letters that speak of the person whom they know, whom they love, and whom they totally support. That is highly unusual in this setting.

"I am aware that these are serious offenses, and I am aware of all the factors that I should take into account including deterrence and that whatever I do may have a consequence with respect to other defendants, but I find it hard in this case to suggest that Mr. Vandemoer should go to jail for more than a year."

What? Now she was saying I should go to jail for a year?

"Sentencing is a difficult task," she continued. "I think it's important to have a punishment because it's too easy to do this kind of thing. Money offenses are easy to do, and it is important for those who do them to understand that there are consequences. Nonetheless, I think jail is not one of them in this case."

I exhaled. *No jail time.* I would be going home with Molly. I wanted to look at Rob but was afraid to take my eyes off the judge.

"I sentence you to a term of imprisonment of one day deemed served, a period of supervised release of two years, the first six months of which shall be served in home confinement with electronic monitoring. You shall pay a fine of $10,000 in such installments and at such times as directed by the Probation Office, and you shall pay a special assessment of $100, of which I have no discretion. That is the sentence of the Court."

We all stood as the judge walked out. Rob smiled at me.

"Great outcome," he said.

Martha Victoria came over and asked us all to meet in the antechamber. My family and lawyers crowded into the little room near the entrance while Martha went over details about probation and what home confinement meant. I just wanted to get outside.

"Can he take his kids to daycare and back?" my mother asked.

"Technically, no," Martha said. "But it depends on the probation officer."

"Well, he has to be able to do that," my mother insisted. My father nodded.

"Okay, Mom," I said. "Let's not worry about that right now. We'll figure it out."

Martha left me with some paperwork. Scott walked in and said, "The prosecution just told me they want to file an appeal. They're pissed."

"My guess is they don't want to do that," Rob said. "We're not a good case for them. They'll wait for the parents."

We all left the courtroom and squeezed onto the elevator. Two reporters jumped in with us. We stayed silent as we rode down.

When we got off the elevator, Rob said, "Want to do this still?"

"Yes." I was buzzing with adrenaline now. I followed him out of the main doors and strode to the microphone stand set up on the sidewalk. Reporters crowded in at my side and in front of me, holding up their phones. I felt my family's presence behind me as I started to speak.

"I'm taking today to take responsibility for my actions, to make it clear what this case is about and finally to move on with my life. A big part of my coaching philosophy has always been it's not the mistake that defines you. Rather, it's what you do afterwards. I'm holding true to those words now in the face of my biggest mistake. I have taken responsibility for my actions and I am accepting the consequences of those actions."

I went on, saying to the press much of what I'd said to Judge Zobel. When I was done, my family and I walked quickly to the Suburban. Reporters and photographers trailed us, jostling each other, shouting questions. All I wanted to do was get inside that car. Molly climbed in first, and I followed. Rob stayed behind to answer questions. The plan was to circle the block and then pick him up.

Molly rubbed my back while I guzzled a bottle of cold water. I'd survived. I'd gotten through it. I didn't know what home confinement was exactly, but who cared? I wasn't going to prison.

That evening, Rob and Scott took Molly and me out to dinner. After we said goodbye, Molly and I walked the long way back to our hotel through the Faneuil Hall Marketplace. It was a beautiful night, mild and calm, even so close to the water. The honey locust trees were fully leafed out, and the air smelled of fried clams and the sea. Cheers were coming out of the crowded bars; game seven of the Stanley Cup finals was just starting.

"Maybe I should get a picture of me in my suit," I said, smoothing both hands over my jacket. "For LinkedIn."

"How about there?" Molly said, pointing to a weathered brick wall.

I stood against the wall and smiled. Molly snapped the picture.

When we got to our hotel room, we scrolled through our messages. We both had dozens of supportive texts from friends and family and colleagues. I didn't want to look at what the press was saying. I'd save that for tomorrow.

"Want to go watch the game?" I said.

"Yes. Definitely."

Molly and I headed downstairs to the hotel bar to join the other Bruins fans. I felt good. Well, better, anyway, better than I had felt in months. This part of the ordeal, at least, was over, and I knew what was ahead of me. Or thought I knew.

22

his thing is weird for me, too, man, I promise you that."

Alton Dural, my new probation officer, was on one knee, removing a device from a hard-sided black case. He was a big guy, at least six-feet-five, with the bulk of the former college football player he told me he had been while he walked around inspecting the Moss Beach house.

"Okay, here we go," he said. He gave me a rueful half-smile and buckled the monitor around my ankle. I wanted to cry.

"You know, my job is to help you get back into society, get a job, right? I'm not here to punish you. I'm here to support you."

It was kind of him to say, but his job was also to tell me where I could and couldn't go for the next six months. "Here's the deal," he said. I could go anywhere that was directly attached to the house, but not beyond it. I could go out on the back deck, but not into the yard. I could stand on the front steps, but not in the driveway. If I strayed even for a moment, say, to take the trash out, I'd trigger an alarm and get an immediate call from the probation officer on duty.

"You can go to work—max forty hours, ten hours commuting— and you can go see a doctor or a lawyer, but you need to submit your schedule online a week ahead of time. You go a month with no problems, you get six hours a week off the monitor. Got it?"

"Yes."

"Okay, man. You're all set." He reminded me I was being billed $3 a day for the monitor.

Nicholas was devastatingly quick to accept my new boundaries.

"Daddy can't get it," Nicholas said to Nora later that day when a ball we'd been playing with rolled off the deck into the yard. "That's okay, Daddy. I'll get it for you."

I had to look away as he bounced down the stairs to retrieve the ball.

When Molly took the kids out on the street to ride bikes, I sat on the front steps and watched. I could see them only when they were directly in front of the house. Nicholas was learning to ride a two-wheeler; Nora was trailing along on a tricycle.

"Daddy, look! Daddy!" Nicholas shouted as Molly trotted next to him, helping him balance. They disappeared from view, then reappeared briefly going the other way. I cheered, but I almost wanted them to stop having these milestone moments if I couldn't be a part of them.

It didn't take long to understand that my home confinement was much more of a punishment for Molly than for me. She had to do everything—pick up and drop off the kids at daycare, shop for groceries, stop at the pharmacy. Plus she was in the middle of running a big camp at PYSF. She was frustrated and exhausted. I was sick with guilt about what I had done to her and the family. I cleaned and cooked and thanked her repeatedly, but nothing I did could make it easier on Molly. The tension in our house was unrelenting. I cried and sulked. I had outsized reactions to little things. Loud noises terrified me. When Molly got home from work, I was eager to tell her about developments in the case; she didn't want to hear it. I hated what was happening between us.

I was still seeing Tamara Hartl, my therapist, every week, and those visits did help some. At least it was a safe place to say what I wanted to say. But even there, I felt I wasn't quite measuring up.

"Why aren't you angry?"

"I am angry," I said.

"But you're not letting that show."

"I don't see the value in doing that."

"Anger can be productive," she said.

I felt like she was right, but I had no idea how to use what I was feeling. It scared the hell out of me.

Plus, I was consumed with the minutiae of electronic monitoring. I had to submit plans well in advance, track all my spending, figure out how many hours I had logged at PYSF and in the car. Since I was new to making the drive over the hill to Redwood City, I often underestimated how long it would take to get there and back. I'd be stuck in traffic on Route 92, the serpentine two-lane road that wound from the ridgetop down to the coast through redwood forests and pumpkin farms, and I'd get a call from the officer on duty asking me where I was.

Coaching, I'd tried to explain to Alton Dural, was not a nine-to-five thing. Helping with Molly's PYSF regattas on weekends often got me dangerously close to going over the permitted work hours. That meant I usually had to skip the race debrief and cleanup.

Just after the Fourth of July, I started coaching a three-day clinic at PYSF attended by sailors prepping for the Club 420 North Americans, an event being held the following week at St. Francis Yacht Club in the city. Before being relieved of my executive director duties, I'd been the one who persuaded the class association to hold the regatta there. Up until then, most of the major 420 events had been held in the East.

I agonized over what to wear on the first day of the clinic. It was hot in Redwood City, definitely a day for shorts. I pulled them on and looked at myself in the mirror. All I could see was the damn ankle monitor. *Just own it. This is what my life is right now. Everyone will have to deal with it,* I told myself, but when I pulled into the parking area at PYSF, my resolve wilted. I knew so many of the kids attending the clinic. I'd even talked to a few of them as potential recruits for Stanford. This was going to be brutal.

I got out of the car, gathered my gear, and headed toward an open-sided tent set up for the event. As I walked across the boatyard, I noticed kids elbowing each other and pointing. I saw them lift their phones in my direction. I tried to keep my eyes forward, determined not to show how uncomfortable I was.

Shortly after I checked in with Molly, a coach came over to tell me that some kids had just posted Snapchats of me and my ankle. I thought it was cruel, but I got it; they were teenagers. I managed to get through the first day. To my great relief, by the second day, the kids seemed to have moved on.

After the clinic, I drove up to the St. Francis Yacht Club to help get the PYSF boats ready. I looked around with pride at how well-organized the regatta seemed to be. Even though I was no longer responsible for it, I still felt like I had a stake in having things go well.

It was a spectacular venue. The Spanish-revival style clubhouse was set on a narrow manmade peninsula near the mouth of San Francisco Bay. The fleet would leave from nearby Crissy Field, a former US Army airfield in the Presidio, head upwind toward Golden Gate Bridge, and then downwind toward Alcatraz Island. The conditions were sure to be challenging; in summer, the bay almost always delivered a big afternoon breeze—twenty knots or more—plus there were powerful currents and tanker ships and commuter ferries to contend with, and fog, of course. It would be a great test for the country's best youth sailors.

I was just about to get a PYSF team meeting under way in the parking lot next to the clubhouse when Dillon Paiva, the association's new executive director, called to me.

"Just giving you a heads-up," he said when I walked over. "A few coaches approached the class about you. They said you shouldn't be here, that you shouldn't be allowed to coach."

"Okay."

"But we told them we disagree. You haven't broken any rule, and you have every right to be here. We told them to lodge a formal protest if they want, but they'd better have a solid argument. It can't just be that they don't want you here."

It was hard to hear, but I wasn't shocked, and I was pretty sure I knew who had complained. The day before, I'd been working on a boat within earshot of three coaches I knew well. I'd heard what they said. "Oh, how the mighty has fallen." "He's just pathetic." "I can't believe he had the balls to show up." I knew they were talking about me.

They never filed a protest.

THOUGH I'D BEEN PUTTING IN MANY hours coaching at PYSF, I still wasn't earning enough to cover our bills. I had to find something else. I combed LinkedIn for leads and applied for dozens of jobs—executive assistants and project managers—but got zero callbacks. By law, potential employers weren't allowed to ask me if I had a criminal record until they were ready to make an offer. But nothing prevented them from Googling my name and finding the nearly thirty thousand hits about me on sites ranging from *Rolling Stone* to the *Japan Times* to *Black Christian News*.

After all the rejections, I was excited to get a message one day via LinkedIn from a man named Kevin Braden, who said he'd like to talk to me about an internship at his company, Next Generation Marketing. The interview was an hour's drive away in Pleasanton, but I was more than willing to make the trip. He seemed so enthusiastic about me. The night before, I received an email with the subject line, "NGM is excited to meet you TOMORROW!" Maybe something was going my way at last.

I cleared the trip with Alton and followed my GPS to a nondescript little industrial park, where the company shared a low, gray building with a judo studio and several loading docks. There was no front desk. Rock music was blaring over speakers. My first thought was that something illegal was going on. I considered leaving. Instead, I walked through a series of doors until I came upon a receptionist. She told me to take a seat.

Eventually, I was invited into a small conference room and greeted by Kevin Braden, a smiley guy in a shiny, charcoal three-piece suit, a dark gray shirt, and a red tie. We sat opposite each other at a table that was too big for the space.

"So, John, let me tell you a little bit about the marketing internship. It's an exciting ground-floor opportunity with lots of room for growth." As he gushed—"Collaborative!" "Revolutionary promotions!" "Hands-on!" "Real-time feedback!"—I began to understand just what this exciting ground-floor opportunity was. He was looking for people to do product demos in big box stores. I had a vision of myself in a cavernous, poorly lit Costco, wearing a hairnet and passing out cheese cubes speared with cellophane-frilled toothpicks.

I couldn't get out of there fast enough. All the way home, I berated myself for being such a sucker. Once again.

My job hunt was going nowhere until my friend Glenn Reynolds called and asked whether he could come over to the house. When he arrived, he said he wanted to officially offer me a job at his company, Water Solutions. He said I would be a specifying engineer, designing wells, distribution systems, water quality testing, and treatment operations to get potable water to clients. I was grateful Glenn was willing to take a chance on me, and I was in no position to turn his offer down. Plus, I thought it was smart to get something on my résumé that had nothing to do with sailing. I accepted the job.

Glenn had a small office in Moss Beach just off Highway 1. Shortly after I started, he left on a long trip and handed me the lead on a big project for the US Fish and Wildlife Service. The job was to design an update to a freshwater delivery system used by scientists based on the desolate Farallon Islands, thirty miles off the coast of San Francisco. I couldn't travel to the site because of my home confinement rules. The seas were often so rough out there that I might not be able to get back on the same day, and I wasn't allowed to be away overnight. Glenn seemed undisturbed by that.

"You know boats," he had said to me encouragingly, as if that would give me the answers to this complex marine engineering puzzle. "Call if you have questions."

I had questions every second, but somehow I got the proposal done. It felt great to have some small success, and when I was engaged at work, I managed to forget for a few hours that I was a convicted felon and that my khaki pants were concealing a black monitor on my right ankle.

After a month of good behavior, I earned a weekly six hours off the device. Alton told me I could choose to use them in two

three-hour chunks on different days or six hours on one day. I chose
Saturdays from 10 a.m. to 4 p.m.

"Take selfies everywhere you go," Alton said. "And turn in all of
your receipts."

I mostly used the time to be with Molly and the kids. We got
ice cream cones, rode bikes, and went to the movies. We spent hours
looking for starfish and hermit crabs and anemones in the tide pools
in the Fitzgerald Marine Reserve, which was less than a mile from
where we were staying. Once, when I looked up and saw Nicholas
and Nora crouched down in their knee-high rubber boots, I flashed
on myself as a little kid with my dad digging for clams in Osterville.
The intensity of feeling caught me by surprise. I had to press my
knuckles against my mouth to collect myself. It was not lost on me
that if I still had my coaching and executive director jobs, I probably
would not be having these moments with my family. I would have
been traveling to recruiting events and regattas.

I used one of my free Saturdays to look at a townhouse we had
rented sight unseen in Half Moon Bay, just south of Moss Beach. It
was the only thing we'd been offered after several weeks of applying
for rentals. In their denials, the landlords had said things like, "Sorry,
it was between you and another couple" or "We decided not to rent,
after all." I was pretty sure, though, that the little "yes" box I checked
on the application next to the question "Have you ever been convicted of a felony?" didn't help our case. With the Half Moon Bay
rental application, I'd attached a copy of a *Wall Street Journal* article
about me so they would see just what my crime had been. The land-
lord said he was impressed with my openness and offered to rent to
us. We signed a lease on a modest, three-bedroom place a few blocks
from the beach.

Even as I was easing into my new job and celebrating the victory of finding a place for my family to live, I still obsessed about the case. I knew Molly would be horrified if she found out how many times a day I refreshed my phone to get updates. It was a kind of sickness. On July 17, I got a Google alert about a story in the *New York Times* sports section with the headline "Caught Up in the College Admissions Scandal: Stanford's Boathouse."

I opened the link with trepidation. There was a large photo of the glass-and-wood boathouse, looking pretty at sunset, and yes, there I was once again emerging from the Moakley Courthouse looking stricken in my new blue suit, with my mother and Molly stone-faced behind me. The story recounted my sins and the ways I and the head rowing coach, Craig Amerkhanian, who had been let go in April for undisclosed reasons, had tarnished the Stanford name and brought a cloud over the gleaming boathouse we had once shared.

July turned into August. Molly was juggling the kids and the shopping and the driving with the massive job of cohosting the three-day US Junior Sailing Championships. I helped her prepare as much as I could, even as I dreaded the competitors' arrival. I knew that among them was a terrific sailor I had recruited for Stanford who would be starting her freshman year there in just a few weeks. Seeing her would be the closest I'd come to encountering members of the current team.

Sure enough, on the first day, I spotted her walking toward me in the boatyard. As she got close, she looked away. It was painfully clear she wanted nothing to do with me. I respected that and kept my distance from her for the rest of the event.

Despite that, being around those kids made me ache to get back to coaching—real coaching. It wasn't enough to just do these random private sessions, to fill in on occasion. I missed being part of a team.

Molly had told me that PYSF parents had been asking for a qualified, full-time coach for the Optimist class. "Optis" are the roughly eight-foot-long, tublike prams used by kids as young as eight who are just being introduced to sailing and racing. When she asked me whether I would consider doing it, I said, yes, absolutely. I thought if I went into the office early and left early, I could get to Redwood City in time for afternoon practices. I'd have to get Glenn to sign off on it, of course, and I'd have to fill out more paperwork for Alton, but I knew I could make it work.

23

In mid-October, a law firm conducting an external review for Stanford trustees contacted me about speaking with them. Rob Fisher was in Los Angeles to meet with a client and volunteered to fly up to San Francisco so he could accompany me to Simpson Thacher & Bartlett, LLC, based in a sleek Palo Alto office park less than a mile from our old on-campus house. Just as I pulled into the parking lot, I spotted Rob getting out of an Uber.

"Remember, you're here as a volunteer," he said as we walked to the entrance. "You can leave at any time."

We were ushered into a conference room where four lawyers from the Palo Alto firm, plus a Stanford lawyer, were waiting for us. Rob and I sat at the far end of a rectangular table. Everyone had two-inch-thick ring binders in front of them.

After some preliminaries, the woman who seemed to be in charge directed us to open the notebook. It was filled with printouts of email exchanges I'd had with Singer, Heather Owen, Adam Cohen, and others. We started going through them page by page. She asked and I answered questions about the messages and various attachments, and about pink envelopes and GPAs and recruiting timelines. I explained it all for what felt like the millionth time. We looked at the résumés Singer had sent me when he first introduced me via email to Molly and Bodhi. Periodically, Rob excused himself to take a call. He was working on a plea deal with prosecutors back in Boston for another client in the college admissions case.

After a lunch break, we dove back into the binder. We talked more about Singer and Molly and Bodhi and Mia. It went on and on. How many different ways were there to pose the same damn questions? Then the head lawyer asked me to turn to a page that held yet another copy of Bodhi's résumé. I saw by the date that this was the one Singer had attached to his June 2019 email when he sent me Bodhi's senior spring grades. I hadn't bothered to open it.

"Oh my god." I felt my face flush.

"Did you not see this?" she asked.

The photograph attached to Bodhi's résumé was of Molly Zhao—or at least the young female sailor Rick Singer had told me was Molly Zhao.

"I, no, no, I didn't. I didn't open this. I'd seen it before, you know, so I had no reason to look at it again. I knew what it said, so—"

"That's not Bodhi Patel in the picture."

"No, it's not."

I felt their eyes on me. Why would Singer have put Molly's picture on Bodhi's résumé? To test me? Had this been part of his grooming process? First Molly's money, then the flattery, the $110,000 gift from his foundation, more fawning, then this bogus photo sent with Bodhi's résumé? He must have assumed I'd seen it and looked the other way, that I had told him with my silence that I was in.

If I had only opened that attachment, I could have said, *What is this, Rick? What have you got me involved in?* If I'd taken a minute to pay attention, to ask questions, it might have changed everything for me.

I braced myself for what was about to come down on me from the lawyers. How could they take me seriously after this? I was afraid to glance over at Rob. Seconds went by, and then the head lawyer asked me to turn to the next page. I exhaled. The group seemed satisfied with my answer; they had seen my shock. And really, why would I lie about any of this now? I was already a convicted felon.

The questioning continued. They wanted to know who else at Stanford knew Rick Singer. Heather and Adam Cohen, I said, and Bernard, I think. I flashed back to that day in the development office when Bernard had congratulated me for bringing in the Zhao family donation and said, "We know Rick well."

"How do you think Bernard Muir knew Rick Singer?" the head lawyer asked.

"Well, I'm not sure actually, but I've always assumed they met at Georgetown when Bernard was the athletics director there."

The lawyer nodded her head slowly. I was pretty sure that everyone in that room knew that Georgetown figured heavily in the college admissions case. Tennis coach Gordon Ernst had pleaded not guilty to charges of taking almost $3 million from Singer and fraudulently designating more than a dozen kids as tennis recruits between 2012 and 2018. Muir had hired Ernst to coach at Georgetown in 2006. Both men happened to be Class of 1990 at Brown University. Muir was not implicated in that scheme and he had left Georgetown in 2009 before the payments had occurred, but I wondered if he knew Singer through their common connection or whether he'd become acquainted with Singer more recently.

She asked whether I'd ever received any training from the university about how to handle donations.

"No, definitely not. No training at all. I think that's something they should put in place going forward. They need a clear policy. It would have helped—" My throat tightened. No. I was not going to let myself cry. "I could have—" I had to stop again.

We'd been at this for nearly six hours. It was torturous, having to go through it all again, having to relive the multitude of ways I'd been made a fool of. The head lawyer looked at me with a sympathetic smile. I was surprised to see that her eyes were glistening with tears.

"So, I think we can agree that what you've told us here today, John," she said, "is that you thought Rick Singer was bringing you recruits, and you thought their families might donate money to your program."

"Yes, that's all it was. I thought I was doing my job," I managed to say. I looked around the room. A few of the other lawyers had tears in their eyes, too.

When we stood, the head lawyer came over and shook my hand. "Patrick Dunkley wanted me to tell you that he appreciates you taking the time to do this."

Once we were outside, Rob said, "That went way better than I thought it would. But don't expect too much. The Stanford trustees hired them."

I looked at my watch. I'd had no idea this thing was going to take all day. I called Alton and told him I'd been delayed.

"No problem, man," he said.

The following Saturday, Molly and the kids and I were planning to take a bike ride while I had time off the ankle monitor. I was searching for the kids' helmets. Nicholas was whining.

"Nicholas, where did you leave your helmet?" I snapped. Nora started to cry.

"Try the garage," Molly said.

"I did!" I said. As I walked, I stepped on a Lego piece in my bare feet. "Goddammit!"

Molly looked at me and sighed.

"You know, I really wanted us to do that hike today," I said. "Can we just do that?"

I'd been pushing to go check out a nearby natural area I'd heard about called Purisima Creek Redwoods Preserve.

"I don't *want* to go hiking," Nicholas moaned. "You said *bike*."

"Stop whining!" I said sharply.

"You know what, John?" Molly said. I could hear she was annoyed. "Why don't *you* just go?"

"I'm not going to go by myself."

"Really," she said. "I think it would be good for you. Go."

I left in a huff. *Fine, then, I would go.* I drove through town and then turned up Higgins Canyon Road, cutting across farmland and then curving up through eucalyptus groves and yellow hills. After I parked in a small lot at the head of the Purisima Creek Trail, I started on foot down a dirt fire road that was littered with yellow maple leaves and lined with tall emerald ferns. I was alone.

The trail narrowed and grew steeper as it skirted a noisy, fast-moving creek. It felt good to be sucking wind; it was the first real exercise I'd done in months. In a while, I entered a sun-dappled grove of rod-straight redwoods and then started across a wooden bridge. I stopped to catch my breath and watched the water below cascade over moss-covered rocks. I felt terrible for being a jerk with Molly and the kids. I would apologize when I got home.

I didn't have a map with me, but I was pretty sure the trail looped back to where I had started. The path climbed and grew dustier, and then I was out in the open in the hot sun. Now there were gorgeous distant views across the chaparral-covered hills to the Pacific. I followed the ridgeline and in a while came upon a couple studying a trail sign. They asked me how to get back to the Higgins lot, and I was able to tell them. They thanked me and walked on. The brief exchange left me crazily elated. I'd helped them out. They were grateful. We had smiled at each other. And they had no idea who I was.

I couldn't wait to show Molly how beautiful it was up here. The kids would love it, too. I turned my face to the sun and breathed deeply. The anger and frustration I'd felt earlier had melted away. Maybe I was meant to be here, I thought. Maybe I was meant to go through what I was going through. Maybe being forced to go "over the hill" wasn't the worst thing. I liked Half Moon Bay. This beautiful wilderness was right in our backyard. I liked my new job and the people I worked with. They cared about me and I cared about them.

I saw it now. Molly and I had been trapped in that Stanford bubble. We told ourselves back then how lucky we were to be living in Palo Alto, where we had the best schools, the best facilities, the best weather, the best, the best, the best. And I had convinced myself that I was killing it, that I was on the way to steering my team to national dominance.

But I think we always knew deep down that something was wrong with all that striving, all that perfection. It was a pressure cooker. It worried us that the suicide rate for Palo Alto's two high schools, filled with bright, privileged kids, was nearly five times the national average. It worried us that Stanford students talked about the Duck Syndrome; the duck appears to be gliding placidly across the water, while beneath the surface, it's paddling like hell. I'd been paddling like a maniac, too. I needed to tell Molly. Maybe Rick Singer had done us a favor.

I started my descent and let gravity take over. I was moving fast, kicking up dust, sending little rocks tumbling down the dry slope, sliding, laughing, having fun. As I got closer to the parking area, I ran into several small groups of people coming up the trail.

"Hello!" I said to everyone I passed. I stopped and took a smiling selfie for Alton. I felt happy, hopeful, thankful, free. I hadn't felt any of those things since before the FBI and IRS agents had come to my door back in February.

I WISH I COULD SAY THAT those feelings lasted, that I'd turned a corner somehow, that from then on, things only got better, but my dark moods returned. I couldn't get to sleep many nights, and if I did finally drift off, I had disturbing dreams about confronting Rick Singer and Eric Rosen. I barked at the kids and Molly. I broke down. I fumed. I managed to function at work, but it took all my will to concentrate on what I was doing. I was jumpy. I felt scared all the time. I missed being the coach. I missed the players. I missed my fucking life. I didn't understand what was happening to me.

And then, in mid-November, my therapist told me I was suffering from post-traumatic stress disorder, or PTSD. I was dumbfounded and a little embarrassed. That was something that happened to soldiers when they returned from savage battles, to people who'd seen and experienced unspeakable horrors. I was a sailing coach who'd lost his job. At first, it seemed ridiculous to stamp my struggles with that heavy label, but the more I researched it, the more I came to see that the diagnosis was probably accurate. I ticked all the boxes. Since PTSD wasn't my therapist's area of expertise, she suggested I look elsewhere for someone who could help me more specifically. She gave me a list of possibilities, but I didn't follow up with any of them. I told myself I'd do it someday.

ON DECEMBER 3, 2019, STANFORD PUBLICLY ISSUED the findings of their external investigation. President Marc Tessier-Lavigne wrote in a letter to the Stanford community that the review had determined that Rick Singer "directly or indirectly approached seven Stanford coaches about potential recruits between 2009 and 2019."

My mind was blown. Ten years? Ten years Singer had been prowling around Stanford? He'd talked to seven coaches, and not one had ever thought to say, "Hey, this guy seems a little shady." The report said the review "found no evidence that any employee of Stanford Athletics . . . [had] agreed to support a Singer client in exchange for a financial consideration" except for me. But I didn't buy for a minute that I was the only one who'd been taken in by him. Why would Singer keep coming back, year after year, if his efforts weren't bearing fruit?

The statement also said that the outside legal review had concluded that Stanford had "no systemic way for concerns about Singer to be elevated and addressed, to ensure increased attention by others he attempted to contact." That I agreed with. To that end, Stanford coaches would now be required to "flag to Admissions and the Office of Development any case in which a recruit came to their attention through a third-party recruiter or consultant and the name of that person."

Stanford also promised that a written policy would state that fund-raising results were not to be considered as part of a coach's performance evaluation. And, there would be "enhanced training for coaches on the fund-raising process and the new gift acceptance policies." I felt a flicker of pride. I'd talked about the need for both of those things when I met with the Palo Alto law firm in October. If nothing else, at least I had contributed that.

My parents and my sister Jennifer timed a visit so they'd be with me during the days leading up to December 18—the date my home confinement officially ended. It rained all week. I was testy. I hated being asked whether I was excited about getting the ankle monitor taken off. The whole thing was humiliating. And I was terrified that something would go wrong, that I'd screw it up somehow, and that I would have to keep wearing the thing. I thought talking about it might jinx it.

On the eighteenth, my parents and sister left for the airport, and I drove to the Phillip Burton Federal Building, a hulking high-rise on Golden Gate Avenue. When I handed the door attendant my ID, he said, "You come in here wearing that?" I was in a Patriots T-shirt. "You're gonna have to turn that inside out for me."

I thought he was kidding, but what if he wasn't? What if this Brady shirt was the thing that would get six more months on the monitor? I passed him warily and got in line to go through a screening gate. When it was my turn to walk through, I put on the conveyer belt the Trader Joe's bag I'd used to transport the part of the device that had been plugged into the wall. The guard told me to go back. I'd set off an alarm.

"Shoes off," the guard said. I went through again. Again, the alarm went off.

I emptied my pockets, took off my belt, and tried again. He shook his head and pulled me aside.

"I don't know," I said, feeling panicked. "I don't have anything on me."

He felt down one leg and then the other. His hands landed on the ankle bracelet, and he pulled up my pants leg.

"You fuckin' idiot," he said, shaking his head. "Why didn't you tell me you had that on?"

Everyone in the line behind me was staring.

"Sorry. I didn't think of it."

"You that stupid? Get outta here."

I collected my belongings and slunk toward the elevator bank. I stepped onto one going up, but as soon as the doors closed, I saw that there was no button for the seventeenth floor, where probation was located. I rode up and back down, then hurried off and searched for an elevator that went to the higher floors. As I ascended, I tried to fill my lungs with air. Everything felt fluttery and strange.

I found probation and walked into a waiting room. A brawny, bald guy with thin black wraparound sunglasses perched on top of his head was at one of two round tables. Beyond him was a check-in window, but no one was behind it. I wasn't sure what I was supposed to do.

"Call and tell 'em you're here," he said, pointing to a phone.

I picked up the phone. The woman who answered said she'd come out to get me. While I waited, I took a good look at the man I was sharing the room with. He had tattoos on almost every inch of his exposed skin, including, I now saw, a large swastika on the back of his neck.

"What prison 'ja get oudda?" he said, lifting his chin toward me.

I didn't want to say I hadn't been in one. Maybe that would piss him off.

"Half Moon Bay." I instantly regretted my smartass answer.

"How was that?"

"Okay. You know," I said with a shrug.

"Just oudda San Quentin."

I grunted. "How was that?"

His obscenity-laced reply led me to believe it hadn't been all that great. I nodded. Finally, a buzzer went off and a female officer came out to get me.

"You're with Alton, right?"

I said I was.

"I've never done this before, so we're going to get a little help," she said.

I trailed her into an office where another officer was sitting at a desk. I felt comforted by the fact that he was wearing a yarmulke. When she told him we needed to get an ankle bracelet off, he pulled some scissors out of a drawer.

"Come on," he said. My heart was banging. I followed them into a conference room. He told me to put my foot up on a chair, then slipped the scissors between the nylon strap and my ankle, and snipped. The device dropped into his hand.

"That's it?" I asked. I had assumed some interior wiring would electrocute me if I had tried to cut the strap myself.

"That's it."

I handed the female officer the shopping bag that held the rest of the device. She said she'd walk me out.

"Must be a relief to have that off," she said.

"It is." I felt so unbalanced I thought I might fall over.

"All set," she said when we got to the door to the waiting room. "Good luck."

I WALKED QUICKLY TO THE ELEVATOR, and once I was inside, pressed myself against the back wall. I felt lightheaded. The elevator lurched as it started down. What if I got trapped in this thing? When the doors slid open on the ground floor, I staggered out. I turned one way, then the other, trying to spot an exit. Everywhere I looked, I saw uniformed cops. I had to get out of this place. I rushed down a corridor and pushed through a double door, half expecting someone to shout, "Halt!"

I'd made it outside. Now I was on a desolate concrete plaza that smelled of urine. A thin plastic bag swirled by me in the breeze. I hurried across the street to the parking garage, fumbled with an entrance door, and then realized I needed to swipe my parking ticket to unlock it. I felt a strange sensation in my throat. *I'm going to lose it*, I thought. *I'm going to die.* I had to find my car fast. When I spotted it, I flung myself into the driver's seat and pushed the door-lock button. My chest was heaving and my hands were shaking. I picked up my phone and called Molly.

"I think I'm having a panic attack," I managed to say when she answered. She talked to me quietly, telling me I was okay, that everything was okay, that all I needed to do was come home now.

MOLLY HAD ASKED WHETHER I WANTED to do anything special on my first evening without the monitor. I told her what I most wanted was to walk to the beach—something I hadn't been able to do in months. After we had dinner with the kids, I hugged her and headed out alone in the dark. It had rained earlier, and the air smelled fresh and green. I walked past houses that had interior lights on. Inside one, I saw a family sitting around a dinner table. *Normal*, I thought. *How nice to be normal.*

At the end of the road, I turned onto the sand path that skirted the coastal bluff. I could hear the waves breaking below. Above me, a million stars pricked the blue-black sky. A three-quarter moon was on the rise. It was so beautiful and so bewildering. *I have to get past this*, I told myself. I had to find a way. I owed it to myself and my family.

I looked down at my ankle. There was a white stripe on my tanned leg where the monitor had been, and in the moonlight, that pale skin seemed to glow. The thing was off, but it wasn't gone. I'd feel it again in the weeks and months to come, surprising me with its phantom presence.

24

On February 26, 2020, I was helping install a wet well on a ranch in the Fremont area when I was startled to see a call coming in from Rob Fisher. It had been months since we'd spoken.

He said he wanted to give me a heads-up. "We just got a letter from Andrew Lelling, the US Attorney. The prosecution is releasing some of Rick Singer's personal notes tomorrow."

"Sorry, hang on a minute." I climbed a ladder out of the open cement vault I'd been in and walked away from the worksite. "You said notes?"

"Yes, years of stuff he wrote on his phone. Some of it while he was cooperating. It's pretty damning for the prosecution."

"Really."

"And the bottom line is because of these notes, you have the right to apply to reverse your plea deal."

"What? Seriously?"

"Yes, although it probably wouldn't change anything for you. They'd come right back and charge you and we'd start all over again. But, I want you to know you do have that option."

"Wow."

I'd been in this position once before when the prosecution screwed up the sentencing guidelines. That, I'd understood, was wildly unusual. And now that heavy door had creaked open again.

"I'm emailing it now. Take a look and then let's talk."

I knew the Wi-Fi signal was much stronger on the other side of the ranch, so I hurried to my car and drove a paved road through open fields dotted with groups of grazing bison until my phone had more bars. Then I parked and opened Rob's email.

The prosecution had turned over about fifty pages of notes Singer had written between 2014 and 2019. Among them were entries made after a series of October 2018 phone calls with parents and coaches, including me. By then, Singer was cooperating, and the government had not only been listening in, but if these notes were to be believed, they were directing him to lie.

"Loud and abrasive call with agents. They continue to ask me to tell a fib . . ."

"I asked for a script if they want me to ask questions and retrieve responses that are not accurate to the way I should be asking the questions. Essentially they are asking me to bend the truth . . ."

"Liz raised her voice to me like she did in the hotel room. . . . This time about asking each person to agree to a lie I was telling them."

Liz. That had to be Elizabeth Keating, the IRS agent who had shouted at me in my house a little more than a year before.

Singer had written a brief entry about one of the calls I'd taken outside my office building when I'd struggled to hear him. He'd misspelled my name. "Spoke with John Vandemoor Stanford Sailing—explained [D'Angelo's] out but I would provide 100–200k to him as requested by the agents instead of the program as I would say normally and reiterated that I [gave] him 500k for Molly."

I felt equal parts rage and relief. Singer was saying what I'd believed all along—that the government had pushed him to drag me deeper into his scheme. They'd wanted him to write that donation check directly to me and to have it appear that the Zhao family gift was a quid pro quo when in fact, Molly had gotten into Stanford on her own.

I called Rob back. "This is incredible."

"It could be a bombshell," he said. But, he cautioned, I shouldn't get my hopes up.

Rob thought the best plan was to sit back while other attorneys dealt with this new evidence. Let the defendants with deep pockets spend their money on legal fees. We'd see what developed.

Sure enough, the next day, lawyers for Lori Loughlin and Mossimo Giannulli filed a motion charging the prosecution with "egregious prosecutorial misconduct" so outrageous as to warrant dismissal of the indictment or, at least, suppression of the recordings. They said the notes showed that the government had bullied Singer into lying to incriminate their clients. They also argued the notes showed that Loughlin and her husband believed they were making legitimate donations, not bribes, to Singer's nonprofit organization. Furthermore, the document's withholding represented a serious Brady violation, that is, a failure to disclose potentially exculpatory evidence.

Eric Rosen responded on behalf of the government, writing that prosecutors had learned about Singer's notes back in October 2018 but had believed them to be privileged information between Singer and his attorneys. When those lawyers agreed to waive that privilege, the government had released the notes. But more to the point, Rosen said, the ramblings of a just-flipped, reluctant witness exonerated no one.

During the next few days, I poured over Singer's entries. In among take-out lunch orders and purchases he may have been considering— "Restoration Hardware Salvaged wood trestle 17th C Monastery,"

"Kymera motorized boogie board"—was an astonishing record of how much money his scam had brought in and how much he'd paid out. And he named names.

Singer also mused about possible new business ventures: sports and performing arts academies, hip-hop dance competitions, international student concierge services, placement services for middle-aged women returning to the workforce. I laughed out loud when I read what seemed to be a plan to produce a line of cookies, to be sold "like the Girl Scouts," door-to-door or through church groups.

"Cremecycle in the middle," Singer had written, adding, "cookies are insane."

He also had weightier things on his mind, including wondering what would happen to him after getting "out"—of prison, I assumed. "How do I have money when I get out? Sell house, 401 K etc Sprinter Van card etc."

And then there were long, reflective entries about his perceived successes and failures.

"I have always been a tad not smart enough, a tad too small, a tad too slow, a tad not as talented but for some reason I have always had a knack for being able to communicate with all ages, races, ethnicities, and cultures.

"Common sense and doing things from the seat of my pants rather than thinking things through and having a plan. Year after year, opportunity after opportunity it seems as if God has selected me to be his messenger and enabled me to engage in opportunities to help despite my lack of knowledge and skill."

Singer had gone on. "Why did I do what I did? How stupid could I be to think I could be Robin Hood! Helping the kids I try to help changed my life as much as I changed theirs. After watching Blind Side on the way home from Boston and after making 15 calls which implicated a bunch of terrific people for their actions that I facilitated—I cried throughout the movie on the plane not because I was sad for hurting others which I was and I take total blame for my actions and decisions but because the one gift God has provided me which is the ability to create solutions and motivate so many to exceed their own personal expectations would be gone for a while. The more I thought about it the more I felt horribly—for some reason God put me on this earth to be his messenger and help make the world a better place but because of my stupidity I will not be able to help those who need the help the most for a while."

I had mixed emotions about what I read. Singer's delusional ramblings made me wonder how I could have been so blind to how crazy he was. But they also helped me understand that his scheme had been sophisticated and complex—and I was not alone in falling for it. I found some comfort there.

Over the next few weeks, lawyers for Loughlin, Giannulli, and other parents still fighting the charges tussled with the government over the notes. My old obsession with reading everything I could find about the case came roaring back. My phone repeatedly pinged with alerts and texts from friends and family who wanted to make sure I'd seen the latest news. All of it fired up what I now recognized as PTSD symptoms. I was sad, teary, quick to anger, sometimes overly animated, sometimes morose. Molly urged me to find a new therapist. I'd yet to connect with one who took our insurance, but I promised I'd keep looking.

Meanwhile, Molly and I, like the rest of the country, had a major new worry—the COVID-19 pandemic. In mid-March 2020, residents of six San Francisco Bay Area counties, including ours, were ordered to shelter in place. Our daycare center closed, and PYSF shut down. Water Solutions stayed open because it was deemed an essential business by the state, but I adjusted my schedule to help Molly with the kids and allow her time to make calls and have video meetings. And once a week, I met with my PYSF Optimist sailing group via Zoom.

In mid-April, Judge Nathan Gorton, known to be one of Boston's more conservative judges, issued a three-page order regarding Singer's notes. The allegations of misconduct by investigators, he said, were "serious and disturbing."

"While government agents are permitted to coach cooperating witnesses during the course of an investigation, they are not permitted to suborn the commission of a crime," he wrote. "In those notes Singer describes a troubling conversation. He indicates that an unidentified agent named 'Liz' and other unspecified 'agents' aggressively pressured him and directly instructed him to lie to elicit incriminating information from potential defendants."

If the notoriously tough Judge Gorton saw a serious problem with how the prosecution had conducted themselves, maybe things were indeed unraveling. I'd always felt this case was not as black-and-white as the media had painted it. It wasn't that I thought Loughlin and Giannulli and others were innocent—I didn't—but if the government had broken rules, their guilt was not the only issue.

Prosecutors filed affidavits from IRS agent Elizabeth Keating and FBI agent Laura Smith. Both had been part of the group that first approached Singer in Boston's Marriott Long Wharf hotel in September 2018 to tell him, essentially, that the jig was up and to ask whether he would cooperate with their investigation. Keating acknowledged in her statement that she was "more animated than usual" at the time because of Singer's refusal to accept responsibility for his crime. Smith recalled Keating raising her voice "somewhat," but added that she was "typically soft-spoken."

Soft-spoken? Um, no. That had not been my experience when

Keating had interrogated me at my kitchen table in February 2019. I flashed on her rising out of her chair and shouting at me, "Don't lie to us!"

The prosecution also filed a just-conducted interview with Singer during which they had asked him to explain his notes. Singer said he'd been referring to arguments with agents about the use of the term "bribes." At the time, he'd considered his clients' payments to be donations. The agents had raised their voices to him, yes. But he wanted it to be known that they had done nothing wrong.

In early May, Judge Gorton ruled that he would not drop charges against Loughlin, Giannulli, or the others, saying agents were merely trying "to get Singer to corroborate, not fabricate, evidence."

Defense lawyers, he went on, would have the opportunity to cross-examine Singer on these points when he had his day in court.

On May 22, 2020, Lori Loughlin and Mossimo Giannulli changed their plea to guilty during a video hearing. Soon after, several other parents did the same.

So, the door had once again slammed shut. I was disappointed. Even though Rob had told me it was a long shot that Singer's notes would affect my case, I had allowed myself to imagine shoving my plea agreement in Rosen's face. I should have known better.

25

O h my god."

I looked over at Becca Carlton, my co-worker, who, because of COVID social distancing, was seated on the other side of the office. Her hand was over her mouth.

"What?" Jacob, our company intern, and I said together.

"I just got a text. Stanford cut men's and lightweight rowing."

Becca had been Stanford's assistant rowing coach until a few years before.

"And eleven other sports," she said.

My heart sank. Jacob found the announcement online and began reading out loud. "'We are writing today with some extremely difficult news . . . Stanford will discontinue 11 of our varsity sports programs at the conclusion of the 2020–21 academic year: men's and women's fencing, field hockey, lightweight rowing, men's rowing, co-ed and women's sailing . . .'"

Sailing. Bernard had done it—had finally swung the big ax. My first thought was that it was somehow my fault, but I quickly squashed that. This went way beyond me.

I searched and found the Stanford press release, too. It had been jointly posted online by Bernard, President Tessier-Lavigne, and Provost Persis Drell.

> Due to escalating costs of operating such a large athletics department, a structural deficit emerged several years prior to the COVID-19 pandemic. That deficit was projected to exceed $12 million in FY21 and to grow steadily in the years ahead. The COVID-19 pandemic and associated recession have only exacerbated the gap: before these sport reductions, our revised forecasts indicated a best-case scenario of a $25 million deficit in FY21, factoring in the effects of COVID-19, and a cumulative shortfall of nearly $70 million over the next three years.

The college's $27 billion endowment, they said, was not available to offset those deficits. The majority of those funds were earmarked for other uses. Even if donors stepped up and raised funds for individual sports, this decision was final.

Later, I found out that Bernard had broken the news to the twenty-two coaches and 240 student-athletes affected by the cuts in a five-minute Zoom call. They'd been blindsided. I was devastated for them, and for all the recruits who would have their pink envelopes withdrawn and their dreams crushed. But I wasn't completely shocked. Sailing and the other eliminated teams, all Olympic sports except for squash, had never been priorities for Bernard. He was all about football and basketball.

And if mighty Stanford—the top college athletics department program in the country, with Stanford athletes winning nearly three hundred Olympic medals—could walk away from those non-revenue-producing sports, I thought it might be the beginning of the end for college sailing at the varsity level. That broke my heart.

MOLLY WORKED ALL SPRING WITH THE PYSF board to develop a plan to offer in-person sailing lessons and coaching with COVID protocols in place. In early summer 2020, I was able to get out on the water with a group of nine Optimist racers between the ages of ten and thirteen. Four times a week, I went over the hill to Redwood City to coach my little team, passing my old turn-off for the Stanford boathouse and continuing to Westpoint Harbor, where PYSF had new headquarters.

It felt important to connect with these kids, given the way the virus had upended their lives. By August, there was even more to fear. Wildfires were devastating communities not far from ours; some days, the smoke was so thick we had to cancel practice. When we were able to be together, I made it a point to communicate with the group about more than just sailing. I wanted them to be comfortable talking about themselves, even if it was only about the littlest things, like whether they'd ridden their bikes that morning or played with their younger siblings. I wanted this to be a safe place for them. It certainly was that for me. No one ever mentioned Rick Singer or Stanford.

When I was done at Water Solutions for the day, I threw myself into writing lesson plans and devising practices. One of my aims, of course, was to help the kids understand the *why* of sailing. I thought if they learned those principles now at their young age, they wouldn't make the mistakes I'd made. Sometimes they glazed over when I talked about resistance and pressure and lift, but more often, I could see their wheels turning and their curiosity blooming.

I also built into my practice plans ways to challenge them. I insisted they rig their boats themselves and launch from the beach, not from the more manageable docks. I encouraged them to figure things out for themselves but also told them that if they ever saw a teammate struggling, I expected them to go over and help without being asked. I wanted them to see that when things go wrong, as they surely will, they are resilient and brave and resourceful enough to make things right.

I was trying to learn the same things about myself.

SEPTEMBER 19, 2020. THE MORNING FOG has lifted. I'm piloting PYSF's red Zodiac up Redwood Creek in bright sunshine, and I'm taking it all in—the glinting water, the cool breeze, the tang of the salt marsh, the line of sturdy prams following me to open water. I'm acutely aware that I have made this trip hundreds of times in the past twelve years with different sailors, different boats.

We leave the shelter of the channel and head into the choppy bay where a steady ten to twelve knots is blowing out of the west-northwest—perfect conditions for what I've planned for today. We're going to practice riding waves. When it's time, I blow my whistle to signal that the kids should turn their boats downwind, then I nose the Zodiac in just behind them so my voice will carry forward. They take off, running free, sails eased out and full. The waves grow as we travel into even less-protected waters, and cold spray crashes over their bows and mine.

I shout encouragement and instructions as the pint-sized Optis rocket along. "Slide back! Move forward! Yes! One pump!"—things I've called out countless times before at Stanford and Navy and St. Mary's; in Chicago, Hyannis, Mantoloking; and at camps and clinics on lakes and bays and rivers.

They're doing great. I can see them making adjustments, weighing decisions, responding to variables. They're getting their boats to plane, keeping their hulls pointing downhill, finding speed, using their bailers when they can, then going back to sailing hard—all the things we've talked about. I motor up next to the group and catch the same wave that is propelling them forward. I hear them whooping and hollering as another swell lifts them and sends them flying. I know they've never sailed in anything like this before. I see their wet, smiling faces. I'm beaming, too.

Eventually, we get to our planned stopping point and turn our bows into the wind.

"That was awesome!" they shout, wild-eyed. "Incredible!"

I'm standing up in the Zodiac, balancing against the swells, surveying the fleet with pride and love. And the kids are looking my way, ready for me to say what comes next.

Acknowledgments

My story would not have seen the light of day if it weren't for Elaine Petrocelli. Thank you so much, Elaine, for all you have done to guide me through this process, including introducing me to Adene Corns, who became my agent and champion. Adene, you are family. Thank you for your support and belief in me, and especially for connecting me with Shannon Welch and the HarperOne team. Shannon, I am so grateful to you for giving me this chance to tell my story.

Meg Lukens Noonan—you have been not only an incredible writer but also a true friend over this past year. You have pushed me, cried with me, and cheered me on. As a coach, I have always believed that the process is more important than the result. I have found this to be so true in the writing of this book and in building a friendship with you. Thank you.

Mark Kelley, thank you for your time and guidance with the project. Your expertise was much appreciated and absolutely needed. Rob Fisher, Scott Seitz, and the whole Nixon Peabody team in Boston—I can't thank you enough for your expertise, your guidance, and your support. You are the best.

My life has been immeasurably enriched by the student-athletes

I have coached. Thank you all for allowing me to spend time with you and for being such a big part of my story.

Clinton Hayes and Belle Strachan—you are both incredible coaches and, more important, incredible people. It was an honor to work with you. I learned so much from you. Atlantic Brugman—thank you for working with me and doing a great job with the Stanford team. You are amazing. A big thank you, too, to Erik Storck and Frank Ustasch for being fantastic coaches in my early years at Stanford.

I also thank Adam Werblow, who has always been a true friend and a mentor. Thank you for being in my corner. And to my other coaching colleagues who have reached out and offered support even when it must have been uncomfortable—thank you.

Through all of this, the Peninsula Youth Sailing Foundation community has been incredibly supportive. I'm so grateful to the PYSF Board of Directors, especially Stephanie Ashworth and Eric Stang, for listening to me and helping me find my path forward.

Anne and Ian Wright—your kind hearts and generosity saved our family and helped us find our way. We can never thank you enough, except to say we will pay it forward and follow your lead.

Glenn Reynolds and Becca Carlton—thank you for showing me a new career path and giving me a chance at a new life.

My sister Ann—I will never forget that April afternoon on the Cape. Playing with my kids meant the world to me. I love you.

My sister Jennifer has always been my partner in whatever we did, from playing in the backyard to traveling around the world to starting our own families. I could not have asked for a better sister. I love you. To my brother-in-law, David—thank you for all your support, kind words, and love. You have blown me away.

Special thanks to my parents, Nick and Sue, for always believing in me and loving me. You have shown me what true courage and compassion look like. Thank you for your guidance, for your love, and for being true to who you are. I love you.

Above all, thank you to my wife, Molly, and my children, Nicholas and Nora. Life hands you lots of ups and downs, but the people you share your life with are what really matter. I know that sounds cheesy, but it rings so true to me. During these past two challenging years, I have grown as a person, husband, and father because of the choices I made; because of the consequences we endured; and, most important, because of my love for you three. I would not have made it to the other side without you. Thank you for your courage and your love. I will always be there for you, and I will love you forever.